MAX DANGER
The Adventures of an Expat in Tokyo

MAX DANGER

The Adventures of
an Expat in Tokyo

by
Robert J. Collins

Charles E. Tuttle Company
Rutland, Vermont & Tokyo, Japan

Published by the Charles E. Tuttle Company, Inc.
of Rutland, Vermont and Tokyo, Japan
with editorial offices at
Suido 1-chome, 2–6, Bunkyo-ku, Tokyo, Japan

© 1987 by Charles E. Tuttle Co. Inc.

Library of Congress Catalog Card No. 87–51178
International Standard Book No. 0–8048–1531–3

First printing, 1987
Fifth printing, 1989

Printed in Japan

For KEIKO
who puts up with all of this

TABLE OF CONTENTS

FOREWORD

by Millard (Corky) Alexander

IT WAS MAY 10th, 1985, that Max Danger first appeared in his knockabout expatriate adventures in the *Tokyo Weekender,* a weekly newspaper distributed to the foreign community who live and work in the Tokyo area. The fact of the matter is that many of the adventures we all experience in Japan are mystifying indeed, and that particular point was the nucleus of the idea that spawned "The Adventures of Max Danger" in the first place. For the foreign reader, who is daily fighting the battle of the plummeting dollar, the soaring yen, and the unending assault of trade barriers and language barriers, Max's frequently baffling and sometimes maddening experiences were, from the first, intended to give heart as well as entertainment.

Since the Japanese work habits, well chronicled in scores of serious-minded books elsewhere, are such as they are, perforce most of Max Danger's adventures occur in the marketplace. Or (equally important in a country where social relationships are on a par with those of commerce) in the saloons and cabarets where top strata businessmen cement the company bonds through saké and beer. With patient direction from

9

his company stalwarts, led by the aptly named Serious Hirose, Max painfully learns the working ways of the joint-venture company, and the pitfalls and perilous pathways in between the acceptable, the admirable and—*abunai!*—the unthinkable.

As if dealing with Serious Hirose, Watanabe-san, and the rest were not trauma enough, Max also has to contend with visits from Head Office executive chieftains whose knowledge of Japan is, shall we say, somewhat less than profound. Numb-headed memos, rockets, and telexes besiege Max, demanding results and business conquests that could only be compared with Danger-san developing the formula for achieving lasting world peace among all men.

In between the chaos of commerce, Japan-style, Max also takes us behind the scenes into the private lives of the expat in Tokyo, with visits from his in-laws, and vacation trips with the beautiful Gloria and the three Danger children. Not any of these excursions (need it be said?) are without trauma and loony-tune denouments.

No, life as an expatriate businessman in Japan is not an easy lot. But different? Well, yes. Fascinating? Certainly. Would Max change his situation? Not on your life.

Robert J. (Bob) Collins, a resident of Japan for a decade or more, has concocted Max's circumstances from certain similarities: he's a top-line executive of a foreign company with many Japanese co-workers and associations. Many of Max's adventures have a true-life connection in Bob's experience. When Max travels as a member of a track and field team, the reader

10

should realize that Bob is himself a top-notch amateur basketball player, was Most Valuable Player as the only foreigner in a Tokyo-wide business cage league, and was named to the all-star team to travel with an otherwise all-Japanese squad to an Asia-wide tournament in Manila. The story of Max's buying Gloria a bicycle for her birthday and the other-wordly difficulties in this seemingly simple transaction also happened to Bob and his lovely wife, Keiko.

And in the most touching account of the death of a New Zealand friend and tennis partner, John Bates, Bob is not only writing about real people, but also saying much about the experience of expatriate living.

In almost twenty years of editing and publishing the *Tokyo Weekender,* I've been privileged to oversee the publication of many writers, columnists, and whimsical scriveners of varying degrees of skill and discernment. Bob Collins—Max Danger—is far and away the most popular series with which I've been associated.

Read on, Japanophiles: you're in for a fine adventure with Max Danger.

INTRODUCTION

Moving to japan can be one of the more exciting adventures ever to engage a Western businessman and his family. Of course, moving to the wilds of Borneo would be an adventure, as would setting up housekeeping on the Lakshadweep Islands off the coast of India, but the frame of reference here is the standard international corporate expatriate relocation.

It goes without saying that moving anywhere is an adventure. London is as unique to Kansas City as Rome is to Madrid. People in Sydney perceive things differently from the folks in Vienna. What works in Toronto or Frankfurt probably won't work in Athens. (In fact, it won't.) Going across the street in Paris can involve major changes in lifestyle. New York City is a foreign country to everyone.

But moving to Japan—Tokyo specifically—involves taking a giant step into a whole new world of social attitudes, cultural beliefs, and business practices. The move entails entering a dimension where time and space take on a meaning conceived of only by science fiction writers and people smoking hand-rolled cigarettes. One becomes the ball in a puzzle which, when the game board is tilted, careens randomly through a maze from someplace to someplace else. And in all senses of the word, the Westerner becomes an alien.

In the Family of Man, the citizens of London, Kansas

City, Rome, Madrid, Sydney, Vienna, Toronto, Frankfurt, Athens, Paris, and even New York are related, in the same way we acknowledge third cousins at a family reunion. We may all be strangers, and we may all notice the peculiar behavior of Mad Uncle Harold's offspring, but we share a recognizable common ancestry—Judaic/Christian ethos, Black Plague, the Industrial Revolution, goat cheese and all.

The good people of Tokyo, however, have shared nothing historically with the West. Nor has the West anything in common with them. Until relatively recent times—essentially since the beginning of the twentieth century—the Japanese may well have been on a different planet. (Or depending upon the point of view, *Westerners* were on a different planet. That, incidentally, may be closer to reality.)

There is nothing profound about any of this. It's just that things in Japan are different. Remarkably different. To pretend otherwise is pure folly. What leads to difficulties are not the differences themselves, but the varying perceptions and levels of understanding regarding the differences.

For example, the initial Level on a Westerner's perception scale clearly indicates a "difference" of great significance. The Japanese speak a language unlike any other human tongue. To compound things, they write the language in symbols that reason alone cannot decipher. The airport customs officers all wear neckties, everyone is in a hurry, and there are long lines everywhere.

Level Two is represented by the sudden awareness that the Japanese are not different at all. Not at all. They ride in elevators, have a dynamic industrial/trade/financial system, own great chunks of the United States, and serve cornflakes at the Hotel Okura.

Level Three is the "hey, wait a minute" stage. The Japanese come to all the meetings, smile politely, nod in agree-

14

ment with everything said, but do the opposite of what's expected. And they do it all together. They really are different.

But *are* they? Level Four understanding recognizes the strong group dynamics, common education and training, and the general sense of loyalty to the family—which in their case is Japan itself. That's not so unusual, things are just organized on a larger scale than any social unit in the West. Nothing is fundamentally different.

Level Five can blow one's mind, however. Bank presidents skipping through the streets dressed as dragons at festival time; single ladies placing garlands of flowers around huge, and remarkably graphic, stone phallic symbols; Ministry of Finance officials rearranging their bedrooms so as to sleep in a "lucky" direction; it is all somewhat odd. At least, by Western standards. There *is* something different in the air.

And so on. Some Westerners, the old Japan hands, have gotten as far as Levels 37 or 38. (Level 39, however, remains a rumor—no one has actually lived long enough to verify it.)

What happens—and this is the theme of the book—is that the expat in Japan must deal with all kinds of people operating at different levels on the perception scale. Worse yet, the expat must deal with people who *anticipate* varying, and often incorrect, levels of perception from the expat. And to complicate matters, the expat can go through a level change in mid-sentence, thereby diluting effective negotiation by the sudden introduction into the conversation of an alarmingly opposite point of view. One would think that painting level numbers on the forehead is perhaps the best solution, after all.

It comes down to this. Newcomers at welcoming cocktail parties are the only people unified in their understanding of Japan. After the first month, diversity of opinion reigns.

15

Consider a Head Office directive written from the "corn-flakes at the Okura" Level to an expat at the "Nude Bathing with the Staff Is Wholesome" Level. One may as well shoot arrows in the dark. The chances of scoring a communication hit are about the same.

Imagine trying to convince a Japanese wholesaler that his problems are understood. The expat may be at the "Belly-to-Belly Communication" Level, whilst the wholesaler assumes the expat still thinks that decorating a stone penis with flowers is peculiar. Relationships begin on tenuous grounds.

And think of the books by Japan "experts" who analyze The Way Things Are. Written at specific levels, they make sense only at those specific levels. And furthermore, that was last week.

Max Danger, Expat, merely makes it through the day.

In the Beginning

"I THOUGHT you said we'd have a maid," hissed the beautiful Gloria Danger, mother of three and new PTA member at three different schools. "The people downstairs already have one, and their furniture isn't even here."

The people downstairs, thought Max, giddy from the effort involved in lacing his shoes for the first of what would probably be a half-dozen times that day, were sent to Tokyo by an R & D firm without a clue as to what it's like living overseas. That fool will probably show up with a driver next.

"Not to worry, my dear," soothed Max, straightening and ungiddying, "we're still prioritizing expenses at the office."

"You're what?" erupted Gloria. Alas, her further remarks were lost as Max, briefcase in hand, stepped into the morning sunshine filtering through the hallway *shoji* in the lobby of yet another Homat—Homat Cornucopia to be exact. It's different for women, mused Max. They spot failed expectations so early in the game.

It had been a long day, and it was becoming an even longer night. Max and two of his business colleagues were visiting a Tokyo nightspot. The pain in his forehead was abating, but it was being replaced by a dull, pre-cramp ache in his legs. Watanabe-san of the General Affairs Department was approaching, for the fourth time, the orgasmic climax of "I Did It My Way" and, at a half-tone below key, he was.

"Head okay now, Dangerous-san?"

"Uh, Danger, and thank you, *domo,* it's much better, *domo.*"

The young hostess was busily fondling Max's thigh and, he noticed with a detachment born of eleven weeks' experience in Japan and a general absence of any feeling from hip to ankle, she had remarkably long fingernails.

"Do many foreigners, er, *gaijin,* come here?" Max asked the pretty girl.

"Heh, heh, many *gaijin* have same head problem, Dangerous-san."

"The name's Danger, and what I meant—"

Applause for Watanabe's efforts exploded, interrupting the meaningful exchange. The young hostess, who only seconds before had been focusing her entire being on Max, led the cheers for Watanabe in obvious ecstacy. What, he wondered, would she do if Sinatra walked in? Probably not recognize him, Max decided.

"Having good time?" asked the respected Mr. Shimizu on Max's left. The question required repeating several times because Watanabe-san's humble refusal to perform another encore was generating cheers from the supporters of the next guy in line at the microphone. The next guy, Max noted, was launching into the same song.

"Oh yes, *hai,* having good time," responded Max, now partially absorbed in helping the young hostess retrieve the candied little pink and white things that had fallen from the table into his lap during the random shuffling of bodies preparatory to Watanabe-san's triumphant return to their group. They were seated uncomfortably on the floor. "Yes, ouch, I find Japan to be very interesting, Mr. Shimizu."

The respected Mr. Shimizu, joint venture partner and closer friend of Max's head office boss than Max himself, had earlier in the day explained at length how maids on the

18

payroll would upset the delicate balance between anticipated sales and controllable expenses—or at least as agreed upon for the current fiscal year. Mr. Shimizu's driver, Mr. Shimizu explained, had already been "projected" from the previous year. That same "projection," added Mr. Shimizu, explained the extra secretary in Watanabe-san's General Affairs Department.

"Perhaps if we could stand up," suggested Max, "stretch our legs, and discuss the maid thing some more—" but the thought was never to be completed. Watanabe-san, flush from his successes at the microphone, and emitting a red glow of radioactive intensity, had over-poured a beer into Max's nearly full whisky and water glass. To almost everyone's surprise and amusement, the agitated foam joined the remaining pink and white things in Max's lap.

"I'm sorry, ha, ha. At least bleeding on your head stopped, ha, ha," Watanabe-san managed to report between spasms that started as giggles and were now both giggles and hiccups. For someone who never spoke in the office, Max reflected, Watanabe-san was a barrel of laughs.

"Yes, head is better," responded Max in a tone that implied an apology to Watanabe-san for having his lap in the way of the beer, and thereby causing that worthy considerable embarrassment.

"*Neh,* Dangerous-san must be very strong," added the young hostess, now thumping a wet cloth in the Danger groin.

"Well, actually, I played American football in high school, but—"

Poof. The lights came on with high noon intensity, instantly aging, by a decade, the formerly young hostess. It was midnight. "Close time," everyone repeated reassuringly and, as if pulled by strings, the customers to a man lurched upright.

19

"You come back again, maybe, Dangerous-san? Maybe we have dinner first," the hostess breathed into Max's ear.

"And use my bottle," roared Watanabe-san between spasms. "Belongs to company."

As was his custom, Max reviewed the day's events in the sanctity of his own bed, lying quietly so as not to disturb the beautiful, and sleeping, Gloria. Having emptied his pockets of extraneous notes and name cards—a mere precaution against potential misunderstanding—Max had noticed that the formerly young hostess was called "Kristie." Curious name that, particularly for a woman from Nagano. He also noticed that somewhere along the way he had picked up a map to the club's sister establishment, Araby Knights, which promised "whisky for fun and sex meetings with song."

A smile played on his lips, only to be interrupted by the flashing memory of his exit from the club after "close time." Banging his head on the doorway going in was bad enough. Smashing it thoroughly on the way out was downright embarrassing.

The smile returned. It wasn't just the recollection of the respected Mr. Shimizu's sudden stomach disorder which displayed itself on, in, and about all the customers' waiting shoes in the club *genkan*. Nor was it the heated exchange between Watanabe-san and the startled driver of what turned out to be a police vehicle—a vehicle against which the leader of General Affairs had sought relief from the tortures and agonies of a full bladder. It wasn't even the terrified cab driver who, spotting pink and white things dangling from Max's beer-sodden crotch, zoomed off into the Roppongi traffic—with the rear door wide open.

The smile was because he had taken another giant step toward figuring out how things happen and how far one can go in the Land of Indirection. Max Danger, Expat, would tell the beautiful Gloria in the morning to hire a maid—and send the damn bills to Watanabe-san, General Affairs Department.

Nice Service

SAY WHAT you may, but there is no place on earth where service is as consistently good as it is in Japan.

Oh, it could be argued that the "greetings" *(Irasshaimase)* and "good-byes" *(Maido arigato gozaimasu)* all shopkeepers utter on all occasions are merely programmed sounds and do not reflect conscious thought. But what a nice thing to program.

It could also be argued that an element of "service" is lacking in a society in which no one is actually able to repair appliances, clocks, watches, shoes, lamps, electric razors, jewelry, home computers, fountain pens, rice cookers, carburetors, compact disc players, intestines, portable radios, typewriters, cigarette lighters, cameras, foreign automobiles, shower heads, stomach disorders, eyeglasses, relationships with Koreans, and/or any other object initially costing less than ¥100,000. (Objects made of wood *can* be repaired in Japan, but that rules out most of the items listed above.)

Nevertheless, the quality and elegance of service in Japan reaches a standard that has all but disappeared in the rest of the world. It is probably due to the fact that Japanese, given the right circumstances, genuinely want to be nice.

Max Danger's first experience in this regard occurred during his second week in Japan. Wandering around the Juban with his eldest child, Max suddenly came all over hungry. He spotted a cozy little restaurant with plastic food in the window. Shrimp, floating in a noodle-laden bowl of brown liquid, looked particularly succulent.

Not knowing what the stuff was called, Max entered the restaurant and signalled a passing waitress. He indicated that she should accompany him back out to the sidewalk. She did. He pointed to the plastic food, pointed to his mouth, held up two fingers, pointed to his son, and ushered the waitress back into the restaurant.

The lady ordered the meals for them, and solicitously concerned herself with their well-being throughout the repast. The fact that the lady turned out to be another customer and not a waitress, and that she happened to be returning from the toilet when Max first accosted her, made no difference. She was genuinely nice. Try *that* in London, Rome, Paris, or New York.

On the occasion of his company's welcoming party for him at the Hotel Okura, Max was particularly pleased to note the attention being paid to him by the lovely banquet girls in kimono. One lovely girl in particular hovered by his side most of the evening. Max ordered a considerable number of drinks from her and an entire meal served on a series of miniature plates. The fact that she turned out to be the wife of a valued client, and not a hostess at all, made no difference. She was genuinely nice. (And she was genuinely embarrassed because Max was genuinely embarrassed when he realized his error.)

Not many months after his arrival in Japan, Max had occasion to consult with the solid citizens managing his neighborhood laundry. Shirts purchased in Korea for the price of a cup of coffee in Japan had a problem with the monograms on the pockets. The initials were backwards. Removing the stitched monograms was probably easier than changing his name to Danger Max.

Max discussed the issue of removing the initials from his shirts with the solid citizens at the laundry. "No problem," it was reported. The fact that the shirts came back from the laundry with no pockets at all is not the point. After expressing concern about that development with the solid citizens, his shirts came back the next time *with* pockets, fashioned from random bits of cloth that almost but not quite matched in color and texture. That's not the point either. What is important is that the solid citizens, confused and embarrassed by the misadventure, subsequently did Max's shirts at half-price until the laundry closed and moved away. The whole thing could not have been nicer.

The most revealing example of Japanese willingness to serve, however, happened during a trip to a resort hotel overlooking the Pacific on the Izu peninsula. Max was saddled with an Important Head Office Visitor for the weekend. The Visitor, Shipley Upman III, knew all about Japan— he was a Far East studies graduate of a small, central Florida agricultural college.

The weekend drill was for Max, the beautiful Gloria Danger, and Ship to abandon themselves to the delights of hot spring bathing, tatami matting, and exotic eating.

All went well. Except for breakfast. "It is the most personal meal of the day," quoted Ship, "and it should not be comprised of things bizarre." His reference was particularly to the dead, black fish with yellow eyes in a bowl of cold weeds. It became the theme of most conversations throughout the morning sightseeing hours.

Ever concerned, especially given Ship's position in the corporate hierarchy, the beautiful Gloria visited with the hotel's kitchen staff prior to retiring for the evening. Bacon,

23

eggs, buttered toast, and coffee were described in words of one or two syllables and appropriate sign language. The staff, once communication was established and comprehension confirmed, could not have been more agreeable. "Western breakfast? No problem. We make for you."

The following morning, Ship, Max, and the beautiful Gloria went to "the breakfast place." The waiters began delivering things bizarre.

"We will have a Western breakfast," Gloria reported to the waitress.

"Ssih," sucked the waitress in reply.

"A Western breakfast, *o kudasai,*" repeated Gloria. The waitress disappeared. She was replaced by a young man— obviously a superior.

"We would like to have a Western breakfast," announced Gloria.

"Ssih," came the reply. He disappeared. An older fellow in a black coat materialized—he was obviously near the top of command in "the breakfast place."

"A Western breakfast, please," requested Gloria. "We ordered it last evening."

The man was halfway into his backwards hiss when comprehension hit.

"Western breakfast! *Hai,* yes, Western breakfast." He positively beamed.

"Western breakfast," he repeated to the younger waiters and waitresses standing in the background. "Ah, *Western* breakfast," they all repeated. Suddenly it was clear. Special arrangements had been made. Western breakfast! Everyone was pleased.

The meal was served in a few moments. Bacon, eggs, buttered toast, and coffee never looked so good.

"Western breakfast, *desu,*" smiled the happy waiter. The young waitress distributed knives, forks, and spoons.

"Western breakfast," she repeated softly.

Fellow hotel guests at neighboring tables watched the scene. "Western breakfast," they seemed to say, as they nodded and smiled at the Dangers and Ship. It was all so nice.

Max will probably remember the meal for the rest of his days. He knows Ship certainly will. The beautiful Gloria, to give her full credit, helped the situation enormously. She ate a slice of bacon from each of the men's plates. She even finished almost all of her eggs. What a woman.

The Western breakfast, you see, had been prepared, as all are in resort hotels, the night before. It was as cold as the grey Pacific lapping at the shores outside the windows of the resort hotel on the Izu peninsula.

Maido arigato gozaimasu.

Company Trouble, Part I

"COMPANY TROUBLE," repeated Max Danger, Expat. "Are you certain?"

"Yes, certain. We having company trouble," explained Serious Hirose, Assistant Section Chief, Department Number Two, Accounting. "It will be next weekend."

Max, nobody's fool, knew that the Japanese tended to organize everything. Even problems were discussed in select little gatherings before they emerged to be confronted by the Group as a whole. Labor demos and train strikes, for example, were planned in advance—often announced in the papers so as not to inconvenience anyone.

"Who else knows about the trouble?" asked Max. Containment and analysis were usually the best tactics. The keep-the-brush-fire-local-before-it-spreads-out-of-control approach to a management crisis, or the business school case book, Case No. 132 solution.

"Everybody knows about the trouble," answered Serious Hirose.

"Everybody?"

"Everybody!"

"I see," Max responded eventually.

The silence in the room as Max and Serious Hirose gazed at each other across Max's desk was interrupted by the tinkling of tea cups brought in by the new girl, a recent Keio University graduate. Max noted that his tea, Japanese green tea, was still being delivered with a small slice of lemon— a misunderstanding dating back to his first day in the office.

"Well, tell me about the trouble and I'll see if we can handle it," Max said after the tea girl had backed from the room.

"No need," stated Serious Hirose, visibly swelling in his chair, "I in charge of everything."

The train rolled in to the little station on Friday at precisely 9:37 P.M. The ride from Tokyo station had taken exactly 2 hours and 21 minutes. No one, Max noticed, had any idea where they were except as how it related to the train line and to the time it took to get there from Tokyo. They could have been north, south, or west of Tokyo—Max ruled out east by himself—but mentally visualizing the location on a map of Japan did not seem important to anyone.

In keeping with the spirit of Max's extremely witty remarks earlier in the week about the employees' outing ("Danger-san pretended he thought Hirose meant 'trouble' instead of 'travel,' and he even pretended to look worried"), everyone now called the trip "Company Trouble." That's a good joke they all agreed—all that is except Serious Hirose, who was oddly silent on the matter.

Emerging from the train, the floor of which was shin-deep in discarded beer and soda cans as well as a half-forest worth of wrapping paper and *mikan* peels, Max looked up at the sky and saw, for the first time since the move to Japan, stars. Finally, he thought, I'm in the real Japan. The Japan of legend. Seven motorcycles roared around the corner, scattering his group.

The *onsen,* or hot bath hotel, was old—definitely not the chrome and steel of Jamaican resorts in James Bond films. Max tagged along with his subgroup of merrymakers as the *onsen* lady led them through corridors, up and down stairs, around corners, and over boards, carpets, and linoleum for what seemed like miles. Max wondered if he'd ever see his shoes again, or indeed if he'd ever see outdoors again. At least Hansel and Gretel had breadcrumbs.

He and his senior staff members were to share a room. Although Watanabe-san of the General Affairs Department was on this trip, the respected Mr. Shimizu, joint venture partner and better friend of Max's Head Office boss than Max himself, had mumbled something about a pressing game of business golf and had excused himself from the "trouble." ("Ha, ha, that was a good one," Mr. Shimizu had told Max that morning. "I got the joke.")

Max knew that a communal bath was in the offing, but the speed with which his colleagues had stripped and donned their *yukata* was startling. An extraordinary amount of underwear was involved in the process, but most were on their way out the door leaving Max still fumbling at the necktie stage. Following, thought Max, is preferable to leading in these circumstances.

Costumed in *yukata,* and flopping along the maze of

27

corridors to the bath, Max lost his slippers twice going down the steps. It's amazing, he thought, retrieving one slipper from the depths of an indoor carp pond: an entire nation of people with feet smaller than mine.

Turning the final corner, Max arrived at the bath area. He knew that the little dressing rooms were separate for each sex. He had read that the baths were often one large pool with a wall down the middle to the water line, also separating the genders. Still, the sound of water splashing and the mingling of voices, male and female, in what must be a large room, was interestingly intriguing.

Max entered the little dressing room, folded his *yukata* and underwear and put them in the baskets provided. He checked himself briefly but thoroughly in the foggy mirror. Clutching his miniature towel, Max took a deep breath. Company trouble, indeed. He entered the bath. Twenty-two naked bodies turned his way. Forty-four dark brown eyes looked at him. All sound in the immediate area ceased.

The tea girl, a recent graduate of Keio University, was the first to scream.

Company Trouble, Part II

RUNNING NAKED from the bath had probably been a mistake. It was the type of "frying pan into the fire" maneuver that has plagued *homo sapiens* since the dawn of time.

Max, of course, had not planned on appearing suddenly in the women's section of the *onsen*. He had, as he reflected later, merely gone in the wrong door. That sort of thing

28

must happen a lot. He should have apologized, perhaps with a bow, reversed his miniature towel and calmly strolled back to his pile of clothes.

However, bolting like a wild man from the nude assembly of his female employees, through the little dressing room and out into the public corridor, was definitely an "into the fire" action.

It certainly surprised the clutch of middle-aged country-side ladies—probably friends since childhood—merrily chattering and flopping their way toward the bath. A lesser man may have been humbled, perhaps struck dumb by the encounter. Not Max Danger, Expat.

"Ohayo gozaimasu," he intoned in his best Executive Language School accent. It was probably the hour, nearly 11:00 P.M., not the intonation that began the interchange.

"Ohayo?" queried several of the ladies at once, seemingly more astonished by the words than his appearance.

No, no, wrong greeting. That means good morning, he realized. *"Er, ikura desu ka?"* Max's feverish brain realized his mouth had just said. It was one of the first Japanese phrases he had mastered, and it occasionally popped out in moments of stress. It means, How much does it cost?

"Something, something, *gaijin,* something," sang out a lady in the rear, apparently addressing the clutch.

"Whoop. Something, something, *okii,*" replied a lady in front, waving her hand in the direction of where Max's miniature towel would have been had he not dropped it along the way.

"Honto, something, something, *shujin,"* another added, immediately setting off gales of laughter. The ladies now seemed to accept the sudden appearance in their midst of a tall, fair, undressed foreigner with unabashed and robust good humor.

"O kudasai," sang the lady in the rear again, this time

29

bringing the clutch to the edge of convulsions. One lady, Max noticed, had to be helped to a chair. The humor in the situation was getting to her.

A hand touched Max's shoulder. The shock of warm, moist flesh on his bare skin produced an involuntary and instinctual reaction—a twisting leap forward. The lady in the chair howled. The others, shrieking, scattered.

"Daijobu desu ka?" asked Watanabe-san of the General Affairs Department, a colleague.

"Daijobu," replied Max. "Okay."

Watanabe-san, Max observed, was emitting steam from the folds of his *yukata.* He had obviously rushed from the men's section of the bath to investigate the commotion.

The ladies crept back.

"Gaijin no something, something, something," the lead lady bellowed. Whatever it was Watanabe-san said in reply set off an explosion of laughter—the type that buckles the knees, brings tears to the eyes, and sends people reeling and bouncing off walls. The type of laughter that can hurt. The lady in the chair rolled forward and on to the floor.

Max turned, unnoticed in the general hysteria, and entered the men's section of the bath. He stayed there until all the men had gone and until all the noise—bursts of more laughter primarily—had ceased on the women's side.

Wrinkled, he slipped into the silent, deserted women's dressing area, found his underwear and *yukata,* dressed, and flopped the long corridor back to his room. Mercifully, everyone was asleep.

Recounting his adventures over dinner the following Monday evening in the beige luxury of Homat Cornucopia, Max's audience hung on his words. The beautiful Gloria Danger hung with skepticism. The lady from downstairs hung with a combination of awe and distaste. Her husband, even newer to Japan than the Danger family, hung with the worldly, knowing attitude that implies familiarity with the pleasures of fooling around naked with a crowd of females.

Max described his departure from the resort, how the countryside ladies all asked to have their pictures taken with him in the courtyard. He described how the husband of one of them, a wizened and bent man with gnarled hands, proudly introduced his sturdy, red-cheeked grandson—a kid of about eight. The kid, who said *"Harro,"* was clearly the first in his family to communicate in a foreign language.

Max also described how, despite the continuous teasing he took from his employees on the train back to Tokyo, no one mentioned a word about "the trouble" on Monday in the office. It was business as usual, as if nothing had happened.

Somehow, Max felt that his explanation was not clear, perhaps not understood. One really had to be there. He decided not to tell his dinner guests about how the tea girl, a recent graduate of Keio University and the first one to spot him as he bumbled into the women's bath, had served his tea Monday morning. The customary lemon slice was decorated with tiny tea leaves, two eyes and a grinning mouth—the happy face. The entire staff, for the first time since the move to Japan, had also said *sayonara* to him as he had left that evening for home. The trouble, Max decided without quite knowing how or why, had been worth it. He looked forward to the next time.

The Birthday Gift

THE BEAUTIFUL GLORIA Danger, mother of three and new PTA member at three different schools, was approaching one of Life's Milestones—her fortieth birthday. The question of a suitable gift for her was something that flitted in and out of Max's consciousness for several weeks.

Many men, and this includes Max, have problems shopping for women. What seems like a good idea at the moment of purchase, becomes less attractive at the moment of giving. Down through the years Max had showered the beautiful Gloria with such thoughtful items as a banjo, bowling shoes, an ironing board cover, and a flame-red negligee purchased late one evening upon leaving a Playboy Club. Good, but not good enough for a fortieth birthday.

The problem of shopping for women in Japan, theoretically easy since shops abound, is exacerbated by communication difficulties. Not only must a gift category be determined—a problem in any language—but the category must be narrowed to a single item by direct negotiation with a sales clerk. The direct negotiation must take place in a vocabulary consisting primarily of *hidari, migi, massugu, kokodesu, mizuwari, hai, domo,* and *toilet wa . . .?*

The solution, Max realized, was to select a gift which by its nature required a display of all variations within the category. Pointing to the desired object would obviate unnecessary dialogue.

And there they were, dozens of them in the store window. Some big, some small, all of them bright and shiny. A complete range of models glimmering in the afternoon sun. The beautiful Gloria's fortieth birthday present would combine all the things one hopes for in a gift—style, performance, originality, and, of course, thoughtfulness. The beautiful Gloria's gift would be—a bicycle!

"We your house deliver," the bicycle salesman announced after Max had made his final choice.

"No," Max explained, "I will pick it up Saturday."

"Okay, we deliver your house before Saturday," the salesman stated.

"No, it's a surprise. You cannot deliver it at all," Max insisted. "I will ride it home. I live near here, Azabu."

"Then we must deliver your near Azabu house," came the reply.

"Look," Max said pointing to the floor of the bicycle store, "you keep the bicycle here. I will pick it up Saturday."

The urge to provide service for customers, Max thought as he paid the salesman, could reach ridiculous proportions in Japan. This guy was adamant, almost in panic.

"But your near Azabu house, where is it?" were the last words Max heard as he left the store.

The distance, as the crow flies, from Kawaguchi-shi in Saitama to Azabu is 32.5 kilometers. The distance, as a tall man pedals a short woman's new bicycle with a big basket on the front through winding streets, up and down hills, and across broad rivers, approaches infinity. Or so it seemed to Max. He had been "on the road" for three-and-a-half hours, and Tokyo Tower, his distant homing beacon, still seemed as far away as it had been at the beginning of his journey. And it was now raining.

Max had arrived at the neighborhood bicycle store precisely at noon on Saturday to pick up the beautiful Gloria's present. His plan had been to wheel the thing up the hill to Homat Cornucopia, hide it in the garage until the dinner party, and then make the presentation between the civilized entree and the low-calorie dessert. The Danger guests would be as impressed as the Danger wife.

The store had disappeared, replaced by a hole in the ground. Workmen were busily preparing the shrouds behind which they would labor mysteriously until a few months hence when there would be revealed on the site something new and magnificent.

It had taken over an hour for Max to ascertain that the bicycle store had moved its inventory to someplace called "Saitama"—a name Max recognized but couldn't really place on his mental map of Tokyo. Clerks in neighboring shops had been quite helpful. Phone calls were made, and the exact location of the bicycle store's Saitama branch was determined. A little note for the taxi was prepared.

It had been early in the ¥4,500 cab ride to Saitama that Max appreciated the extent of his problem. For the first ten minutes he watched the passing scene carefully—memorizing intersections, signs, and corner buildings. But wherever Saitama was, it wasn't near Azabu. It turned out to be far, far away.

Now, pedalling through the rain in impending darkness, Max began to recognize familiar scenes. Book stores, the Russian restaurant. Kanda! If the reckoning was correct, the Palace was dead ahead. Only an hour or so more to Homat Cornucopia. Whew!

Little things in life cause the greatest problems. Little things fuel the flames of frustration. Max had not been angry over his arrest in Kanda. Clearly, lightless night bicycling *is*

34

wrong. Furthermore, aliens without registration cards on their person *are* in contravention of the laws of the land. (Max's booklet was securely stashed in yesterday's suit.) Shackling the new bicycle to a pipe in the police box was merely a matter of expediency. The police car ride to Azabu, far from being annoying, was actually rather pleasant. Even the dramatic entrance to the Danger apartment in the midst of beautiful Gloria's birthday party—Max soaking wet and flanked by two of Tokyo's finest—did enliven the proceedings.

There were puzzled looks and incredulous remarks to be sure, but Max, having satisfied the police that he was not a Korean gangster, carried off the remainder of the evening rather well. He had no present for Gloria, of course, but the promise of wonderful things on the morrow, coupled with his mysterious activities of that day, led to the kind of speculation that keeps a party going.

No, none of the above was particularly annoying. If anything, Max was more embarrassed than angry over his misadventures. What was annoying—what kindled the flames of frustration to the point of rage—was his trip back to the Kanda police box on Sunday morning. The bicycle, shackled the night before to a pipe, was gone.

The police, ever helpful, had arranged to deliver the bicycle—back to Kawaguchi-shi, Saitama, a distance of 32.5 kilometers from Azabu, as the crow flies.

Golf Play

THERE ARE PEOPLE on this planet who enjoy a round of golf. And there are people who don't.

Max Danger, Expat, was in the former category. Walking around with a group of pals in the sunshine, chasing a ball up and down hills for a few hours, and then having a bunch of beers in the club house with the day's activities under review is fun. ("I was five over par until the 15th, but that's when the water buffalo swallowed my ball and my caddy. I came apart after that and quadruple-bogied the last four holes. Another round of beer, please.") Ah, it's great, and it sure beats sitting in the office wearing a necktie.

There is, however, a third category of people on this planet. The people in the third category are called "Japanese." Walking around hitting a ball is merely incidental to the overall adventure involved in Golf Play. Getting there, whatever the effort; starting, whatever the weather; finishing, whatever the course conditions; and going home, whatever the traffic, create a "come hell or high water" approach to having fun. Max's time had come. He was scheduled for Golf Play on the weekend.

The blood, dripping off the end of Serious Hirose's nose and on to the shank of his putter, down which it ran to dribble on and about his potential par four lie, did not appear to disturb him in the least. The fact that the torrential rains immediately washed away all traces of Hirose's precious bodily fluid was probably a factor, thought Max.

Watanabe-san of Max's General Affairs Department and 'Mike' Morimoto, Valued Client, leaned into the wind and watched in silence. ('Mike' Morimoto had been stationed in New York for 18 months in the early '60s. 'Mike' was 'Mike' to any American acquaintance. 'Mike' was Morimoto-shacho to his close Japanese friends.)

Hirose sank the putt and fainted.

"That's the third time he's done that," complained Watanabe-san, referring to the fainting, not the putting. "I apologize," he added, bowing slightly to the Valued Client.

"No problem," replied 'Mike' good-naturedly. "Let's just drag him under those trees."

Max, carrying Hirose's ankles so as not to damage the green, observed that although unconscious, Hirose was still shivering. Laying Hirose under a tree, Max straightened and realized he was the one shivering.

"Maybe we should quit," Max suggested, by now knowing the probable reply.

"No," replied Watanabe-san, "only one more hole to go. Hirose will be okay in a minute."

Serious Hirose's problem actually began the night before. In order to begin Golf Play at 7:00 A.M., Max's group journeyed by train the previous evening to a small inn near the course. After a sumptuous meal of curry rice and steamed weeds, the foursome was entertained and amused by a grandmotherly lady dressed up as a geisha. A great deal of beer was involved. One minute Hirose was standing erect, the next minute he was face down on the floor—his nose striking first from a height of 5 feet 4 inches. Max had wanted to call off Golf Play then, but he lost the vote 1 to 3. Hirose had been bleeding, more or less, ever since.

The trip in the morning from the inn to the golf course—

a trip conducted by a local cab driver who lost his way in the fog and rain—added to Max's misgivings. After the cab went off the road and settled in a rice paddy, the activity involved in retrieving the clubs from the cab's trunk meant standing knee deep in muddy water. Max lost *that* vote to cancel Golf Play 1 to 3 also.

Now, huddled under a tree watching a 75-year-old caddy person lady pour a vitamin C drink down Hirose's throat, Max expressed concern about Hirose's color—blue.

"Ho, ho," laughed Watanabe-san and 'Mike' together. "You look worse," 'Mike' added.

As if on cue, Hirose blinked his eyes open, sat up, wiped his nose on his sleeve, asked Max if he was okay, struggled to his feet, and said, "Ret's go."

They finished the last hole with nothing more remarkable happening than 'Mike's' fall into the lake. They had all driven badly on that hole—the storm had blown a large tree down immediately in front of the tee area. A higher club than normal was required to loft the ball over the barrier of branches and crushed greenery. The gale force wind blew all the balls to the right, giving Max, a confirmed hooker, the first slice of his life. It gave 'Mike,' a slicer, a trip to the lake's edge. He fell in when Max shouted "Be careful" at him. Hirose four-putted, fainting again briefly between the second and third putt.

Max squirmed in his club house chair. The after-golf bath had felt good, but putting wet underpants back on ranks somewhere between acute nausea and death as a physical sensation. It is possible for a rash, Max noted, to develop within seconds.

But Max's wet underpants had nothing to do with his chair squirming. At the Valued Client's suggestion, a vote was being taken. The issue was whether or not to stay in the inn one more night, and to do some more Golf Play the next day.

The vote was 1 to 3.

The Head Office Visitor, Part I

"WILL ARRIVE APRIL 26 FOR ONE WEEK. MAKE NECESSARY ARRANGEMENTS AND FORWARD SUGGESTED ITINERARY—HOLSTEIN"

"SURPRISED AND HONORED TO LEARN YOUR JAPAN VISIT. BE ADVISED WE HAVE GOLDEN WEEK (MEANING CLUSTER OF NATIONAL HOLIDAYS) DURING THAT PERIOD AND MOST JAPANESE VACATIONING. MIGHT SUGGEST FOLLOWING WEEK AS BEING EVEN BETTER FOR TRIP—DANGER

Max Danger, Expat, had worked for Bartholemew ("call me Bart") Holstein for nearly 15 years. To be more precise, Max had worked for people who worked for Bart for 15 years. Max, in fact, had only met the Great Man twice. (The second meeting was on the eve of Max's departure for Japan. Bart's advice was, "Give 'em hell and don't take 'no' for an answer." Max had yet to hear "no" for an answer in Japan.)

Holstein, CEO of a vast and powerful conglomerate, was described in business journals as one who "combines the determination and drive of all successful executives with an almost avuncular concern about the 'people' side of the equation." Holstein was even becoming known as a philanthropist of sorts. He was pictured in *Time* magazine at a charity ball. He liked animals—polo ponies particularly. His response to Max's suggestion was brief:

"CANCEL GOLDEN WEEK—HOLSTEIN
P.S. WIFE WILL ACCOMPANY ON 26TH"

"He doesn't travel well," Max's Immediate Head Office Supervisor explained during the 3:00 A.M. (Tokyo time) phone conversation. "And his wife hates cigarette smoke."

Christ, thought Max, lighting a cigarette in the dark, so do I.

"But Ship will go to Tokyo a few days in advance," continued Max's boss, "to help with arrangements."

Every large company has a "Ship." In Max's company it was Shipley Upman III, grandson of a corporate founder and inheritor of an obscene amount of stock. He was a Far East Studies graduate of a small, central Florida agricultural college. He was Bart's right hand man on all things Oriental. He thought the bullet train went from Tokyo to Hong Kong.

"Ship couldn't arrange a gang-bang in a penal colony," Max declared, hoping panic didn't register in his voice.

"That's not the point," replied the boss. "If Bart thinks he can help, he can help."

"Are these real cornflakes?" Ship asked Max on the morning of his third day in Tokyo. Breakfast at the Hotel Okura invariably produced the first of what would be by the end of the day a series of rather remarkable questions from the scholar of Far East Studies. On the previous day, Ship had wondered aloud during a meeting with the staff if the Prime Minister could be invited to the office to meet Bart. Ship had asked Serious Hirose, of Company Trouble fame, if one could see where "the atom bomb hit" from Tokyo Tower. Ship had asked Watanabe-san of General Affairs what he had done during the war. Ship had asked the lady cleaning the toilets if she realized that the gold in her teeth was decreasing in value each day. (On his first trip to Japan, a few months earlier, Ship had asked the owner of a resort hotel if the "terrible food" was responsible for all Japanese being "scrawny.")

"Those are real cornflakes, Ship. American," Max added.

It had not been easy, Max reflected. Particularly with Ship around. But the following had been arranged so that Bart's visit beginning the next day would maximize his exposure to both the country and the people, while at the same time provide the Japan operation with whatever benefits his presence might produce. Blackmail, cajolery, diplomacy, pleading, and emotional bribery had been among the techniques employed.

1. The Tokyo office key staff had been persuaded to forego golf, tennis, family outings, visits to native places, and sleep-ins so as to be ready to meet with Bart during Golden Week.
2. The respected Mr. Shimizu, joint venture partner and better friend of Max's boss than Max himself, had been persuaded to produce his wife, until now a mythical woman, at a cocktail party hosted by the beautiful Gloria Danger in honor of Holstein's wife.
3. The beautiful Gloria Danger had been persuaded that a new Issey Miyake fashion ensemble was not necessary for the cocktail party.
4. A banquet room at the Tokyo American Club had been booked, invitations sent, and personal phone calls made to two hundred businessmen begging participation.

41

(The I-went-to-your-damn-party-you-must-come-to-mine approach to the situation.)

5. A medium-to-high ranked MITI Official, paying off mah jong debts to a classmate in Max's office, had agreed to "receive" Bart for a discussion on U.S.-Japan trade matters.

6. A trading company official—a potential distributor— was persuaded to return from his labors in Bangkok two days early for a meeting with the Great One.

7. An American Chamber of Commerce Briefing Breakfast had been arranged on Saturday morning—the first in history—to provide Bart with a panel of experts with brains to pick.

8. Usurious fees were paid in advance for short-notice booking of rooms at a Kyoto Japanese-style inn. Cars had been hired to handle related transportation, at rates approximating their trade-in value.

9. All smokers were alerted and warned of the fact that their fumes might send Mrs. Holstein into hysterics.

10. The Danger family vacation arrangements in Guam were cancelled, sending two of the three children into hysterics.

Max, with Ship in tow, went to the office. There had been a minor delay at the Okura whilst the breakfast bill was being settled. Ship had asked the cashier if she was married "to a Japanese." The answer, which was "yes," took awhile—the cashier never having been asked that question before.

The telex from the Head Office was eloquent in its brevity.

"TRIP POSTPONED. RE-SCHEDULE FOLLOWING WEEK—HOLSTEIN"

The Head Office Visitor, Part II

SPRING IN TOKYO can be glorious. Between the gray chill of winter and the blast-furnace heat of summer, spring's warming sun and gentle breezes make the entire year worthwhile.

It is a sensual time. Trees and bushes, unnoticed otherwise, blossom and bloom in a riot of color. The tan grass greens. Fishmongers, noodle vendors, yakitori purveyors, and beer hallers add their special sounds and odors to the passing scene.

Spring is the time for strolling. Scurrying belongs to the rest of the year. Lovers touch. Young girls, in the latest of current fashions, parade. Every corner and byway presents the promise of adventure.

It is the best time of the year for tourists and visitors. Minutes, among the streetside wares of shopkeepers and merchants, become hours. Anybody would be intrigued.

Unless, of course, it rains.

"I've never seen so much goddam rain in all my goddam life," reported Bartholemew ("call me Bart") Holstein, Chief Executive Officer of one of America's most powerful conglomerates. "If I'd known it rained so much in Japan," Bart added in the voice that regularly negotiated million-dollar deals, "I'd have sent in my place a goddam duck."

"Good point, sir," confirmed Max Danger, Expat and

host of his boss' boss' boss on the occasion of his first Tokyo visit. "But at least it's not the 'rainy season'."

Mrs. Holstein, a giggler, at least when not choking on real or imagined cigarette smoke, giggled.

"That's not funny," Bart pronounced. "Either of you."

The Head Office visit was not going well. Standing in a downpour on the platform of a train station somewhere in the environs of the Tsukuba International Business Exposition, Max reflected on the events of the past week.

1. Although the room at the Hotel Okura was certainly magnificent by Max's standards, the absence of a full kitchen—for the personalized preparation of Bart's special diet of curds, whey, and stewed tomatoes—seemed to throw the Great Man off his reputedly stable equilibrium.

2. The meeting with the MITI official, arranged under duress and without the enthusiastic support of the official himself, should not have degenerated into a lecture highlighting the deficiencies of Japanese corporate/political/social/economic principles as compared to the virtues of American free enterprise and capitalistic adventurism.

3. Max's office, too goddam large by "corporate standards" with only Bart and Max in it, had become too goddam small once the first staff meeting was convened.

4. The American Chamber of Commerce Briefing Breakfast—the first in history scheduled on a Saturday morning—should not have been skipped in favor of a visit to the fish market (which in turn was skipped because of rain). Max's Chamber peers were already threatening a committee chairmanship appointment in retaliation.

5. The non-appearance of Mt. Fuji during the train ride to

44

Kyoto had been linked somehow to Max's organizational abilities, or lack thereof. ("You said we'd see the goddam mountain," Bart had accused. "A little rain doesn't make a goddam mountain invisible.") The non-existence of beds in the Japanese-style inn had been even more disconcerting. ("Get 'em in here right away," Bart had suggested. "I'm not sleeping on the goddam floor.") Bart, nevertheless, ended up on the floor, but had awakened the next day in a particularly foul mood. ("That's not a goddam castle, that's just a wooden house on a hill.")

6. The cocktail party, arranged by the beautiful Gloria Danger in honor of Mrs. Holstein, was a particularly unfortunate affair. Mrs. Holstein, it developed, balanced her intolerance for tobacco smoke with an inordinate fondness of demon rum. To say that her social judgement was impaired is perhaps too moderate a statement. Ordering repeated refills of drinks from the kimono-clad wife of the respected Mr. Shimizu—joint venture partner and better friend of Max's boss than Max himself—could perhaps be excused on the basis that banquet hostesses are often the only ladies still dressing in the traditional style. But falling asleep suddenly whilst hovering over the cheese dip created the type of disturbance that is difficult to explain, or ignore.

Even the events leading to the current situation—standing on a remote train platform in the driving rain—were unhappily awkward. The Holsteins wanted to see Tsukuba. Max arranged a car and driver. The Holsteins wanted to go by helicopter. Max cancelled the car and driver. The weather cancelled the return helicopter flight. Max suggested the train. The more impatient Bart became, the more Mrs. Holstein giggled. Things were deteriorating, but Max

45

promised that they would be in Tokyo within the hour.

The train roared into the station. Its doors yawned, passengers boarded. Doors closed, the train roared off, Tokyo-bound.

Max Danger, Expat, Bart Holstein, CEO of a major American conglomerate, and the giggling Mrs. Holstein watched the train recede in the distance. Max wondered where his next assignment, if any, would be. They had been on the wrong platform.

Max lit his first cigarette in a week.

The Bad Day

THE TELEPHONE POLE, against which the cab driver was urinating, began to sway—gently at first, but in an ever increasing arc. It broke from its foundation a foot above ground with an ear-piercing crack as metal parted metal. The swooshing sound of wires being dragged through the branches of surrounding trees, accompanied by popping and sparking as the wires snapped, preceded the kerthud-tinkle of the pole cleaving the empty taxi. A cat screeched.

The cab driver, adribble, stood transfixed. A steaming puddle gathered at his feet. Leaves, twigs, and small branches rained down upon him. The air in his lungs, collected moments earlier for the last bars of a lovely *enka* tune, burst out in a scream that rang through the black Azabu night. He turned, casting modesty aside, and ran. His screams could be heard all the way down the hill, past the Juban, and up beyond the Australian Embassy.

Max Danger, Expat, awoke with a start and turned off the wailing alarm. Only two kinds of dreams left a smile on his face, and this was one of them. It was going to be a good day.

But, alas, the Grand Scheme of Things often dictates otherwise. There really are good days and bad days. This balance gives life the special tang that separates it from other forms of existence. Stones don't have good or bad days. Suffering enhances pleasure which in turn makes poignant the sadness that magnifies joy. And so on.

Getting out of bed Max stepped on the cat's tail, this time in his bare feet. The bleeding didn't stop until well after the 8:00 news. It was *not* going to be a good day.

"Your company has license to *manufacture* the cooker domestically," explained the Ministry official with the patience one employs to describe advanced physics to a four-year-old. "But your company has no license to *sell* the cooker domestically."

The Home Appliance Division of Max's conglomerate employer—an operation that had been ignored for years—was now being brought back to life. Max was receiving directives to resurrect the half-forgotten plan to manufacture and sell rice cookers to the Japanese.

"And do not know if Japanese people can accept taste of rice from your cooker," continued the official.

"But that's why we wish to test market the product first," said Max. His company colleagues, offering moral support and interpretation on the trip to the Ministry, nodded in unison.

"I already explained you cannot test market until license to sell," confirmed the official. "Japanese people may not like taste." Max's colleagues again nodded in unison. The reasoning was impeccable.

The "seeking administrative guidance" session was over. Deep bows were performed. Max, limping slightly, and his colleagues walked in silence through the dusky corridors of the Ministry. They reached their waiting car.

"Rice cooker kind of sandwich to Newcastle, don't you think?" offered Max's Engineering Department Manager, Muzukashi-san.

"Or coals to a banquet," added Max glumly.

Entering the car, Max slammed the door on his right index and middle fingers.

Fishing shabu-shabu from a boiling cauldron with chopsticks at a luncheon hosted by a supplier is impossible to do left-handed if you are normally right-handed. Max drank the soup.

Importing baking dough from the States seemed like a good idea to Max. Not only had he found a Japanese distributor for the stuff, he had made a hero of himself to the guys in the Head Office: Food, Beverage and Industrial Paint Division. It was their inaugural order in the Orient. Notification of the arrival of the very first shipment was made to Max as he returned, limping and still hungry, from lunch.

Because the dough must be shipped frozen, Max's instructions clearly indicated that the shipping temperature could not vary from the acceptable range of 29°F to 32°F. The people in the Food, Beverage and Industrial Paint Division certainly understood this. However, somewhere along the line a shipper decided that since Japan operates on the Centigrade instead of the Fahrenheit system, the dough should be shipped at 32°C.

What arrived at Yokohama was a forty-foot long, twenty-foot high, expanding-by-the-minute, loaf of bread. Dock workers were concerned about an imminent explosion that might engulf the port in American wholesomeness. Max ordered the stuff dumped into the ocean. An hour later the insurance company people called to report that they would not entertain a claim unless they could examine the damage first.

The beautiful Gloria called at 4:00 to announce that their oldest child, the one whose ¥750,000 braces were removed the day before, had taken a nose dive over his bicycle handlebars and had broken off his front two teeth at the gums.

The beautiful Gloria called at 4:30 to announce that whilst en route to the dentist's office, she ran the Danger Honda into the side of an American luxury car driven by a chunky Japanese man with curly hair, and missing fingers, who was dressed in a white suit, black shirt, lavender tie, and a pair of wooden clogs.

The telex machine broke down in mid-transmission of Max's carefully worded telex to the Head Office regarding the rice cooker escapade. That meant a 3:00 A.M. phone call from New York would be on its way.

Taking taxis, Max thought during the trip home that evening, is actually a convenient and rather civilized aspect of Tokyo life. Of course one must get past the "destination unknown" phase:

"Hiroo, *onegai shimasu.*"
"Hiroo?"
"*Hai*, Hiroo."
"Hiroo, *nan desu ka?*"
"Hiroo!"
"Hiroo?"

"Hiroo!"

"Ah, Hiroo!!!"

"*Hai,* Hiroo."

Reviewing the events of what really had been a bad day, Max wondered if the family would "buy" the suicide theory if he were to fling the cat off the roof of the building. He wondered if the Ministry official had read *Catch-22*. He wondered if any of his fingers were broken. (He wondered if he could take his contact lenses out left-handed.)

The taxi swerved around another taxi that had stopped suddenly in the middle of the street. Max wondered if his heart would start again. He also wondered if a loaf of bread the size of a three-bedroom house would be a navigation hazard to ships at sea. If so, would he be blamed?

The taxi pulled up at Homat Cornucopia. Max paid the man. He limped up the front steps, now wondering how his oldest felt. Losing front teeth at this age will not appear to be the problem it becomes later after years of partial plates, caps, bridges and other oral machinery.

Max looked back at the taxi. It was still there. The driver was urinating against the telephone pole across the street. Was this the dream? Max blinked. The driver was still there—in fact, he was humming an *enka* tune.

Max was almost afraid to look at the pole to see if it was swaying. He finally looked. It was not.

The scream was the same, however. Max later swore he also heard a cat screech. Unlike the dream, there were pedestrians around. Also unlike the dream, the driver didn't run. He fell to his knees, doubling over so that his head touched the ground.

Max had been so impressed by the event that he made an effort to find out a little about the man. His name was Matsunaga Hiroshi of Musashino-shi, and he worked for Daiwa Cab Company, driving taxi number 45. He was newly married, and had spent his honeymoon in Guam two weeks before.

Matsunaga Hiroshi had suffered a most vicious assault to his private parts. He had been stung by a bee.

You talk about bad days.

The Day More People Came Down Mt. Fuji Than Went Up

CLIMBING MT. FUJI is an activity that dates no doubt to the earliest inhabitation of Japan. It has been climbed for many reasons—as a religious experience, for recreation, as a personal challenge, and because it's there.

Thousands make the trip to the top each year. Blind people do it, people in wheelchairs (with considerable assistance) do it, octogenarians in *tabi* do it, office ladies do it.

Bicycles, pets, and infants have been dragged to the top. Self-Defense Force squadrons, in full combat gear, actually *jog* up the thing.

Any club or organization worth its salt in Japan schedules regular pilgrimages to Fujiyama. A man in Gifu claims to have climbed it 106 times. (One wonders what he does with his branded sticks.)

The day arrived when Max Danger could no longer ignore the lure of the ultimate outdoor Japan experience. One sunny Saturday morning in the middle of July, Max and three friends decided to "conquer the brute." It turned out to be an historic expedition—at least historic in living memory. (God only knows what our early ancestors were

51

up to.) It was The Day More People Came Down Mt. Fuji Than Went Up. Max, and probably quite a few folks on the slopes that day, will never forget it.

Max's companions were Ted Miyabe, an American-born *sansei* whose knowledge of Japanese consisted of the single word, *sayonara,* George O'Leary, a visiting former grade school classmate of Max's, and Dr. Horst Meyer, O'Leary's German brother-in-law.

Interestingly, Dr. Meyer spoke *no,* repeat *no,* English. He was emphatic about that. O'Leary and his brother-in-law, on a world trip together, communicated in O'Leary's baby-talk German. O'Leary had always been, Max reflected, bad at languages.

Given the circumstances Max, in the *hidari, migi, massugu* mode for taxi rides, was the group's interpreter. (Unless, of course, they were leaving somewhere, in which case Miyabe would contribute a *sayonara.*) The quartet was on shaky ground in the area of accurate or precise communication. Natives only spoke to Miyabe.

Things began badly. Suitable clothing could not be found to fit Dr. Meyer. He finally settled upon madras bermuda shorts from O'Leary's luggage, his own black dress shoes and brown socks, a slick nylon see-through short-sleeved shirt—the kind that reveals one's taste in underwear—and the beautiful Gloria Danger's pink sweater with fluffy balls dangling from strings "down the bodice."

O'Leary wore the pin-striped vest to his business suit over a sweatshirt, Max's tennis shorts and tennis shoes, and carried his Harris tweed top coat.

Miyabe, a duck-hunter, wore his duck-hunting costume—and looked lost. He was a symphony in dull green.

Max wore his ski outfit, and was hot for 95 percent of the trip.

Taxi drivers, not comfortable with "the fifth station at

Mt. Fuji" as a direction, began to play hunches as to where the foursome was *really* going. (Their first driver took them to Shinjuku. The next driver took them to Omote Sando.)

They finally made it to the fifth station, but plans to go up the mountain and back down by nightfall were scrubbed. It was three o'clock in the afternoon, and the "seeing the sunrise" climbers were just beginning. What the hey, said Max's group, we'll go ahead and spend the night "up there." Fate had a Hand in all this.

The climb, as many know, is an ordeal. Loose rocks and empty Orange Plussy cans make the footing treacherous. Max's party tended to ascend in spurts—twenty minutes of climbing, five minutes of resting. Climbing and resting, at higher altitudes, began to approximate each other in time.

Max reckoned he passed the same old lady on six occasions. She smiled sweetly at Max whenever *she* passed *him* during his "resting" phase. She never seemed to stop. Max began to hate her. (Old ladies should not be permitted on Mt. Fuji.)

It was dark when Max's group hit the eighth station. Apart from having the smelliest toilet (in the eye-watering category) on planet Earth, the facilities were unremarkable. A large wooden hut, with a basic (hot soup) kitchen and a comfortable wooden floor, greeted the hearty adventurers.

There was, by any reasonable estimate, room for about fifty people in the place. There were, by conservative estimate, two hundred hearty adventurers in the place. *"Daijobu,"* said the red-cheeked lady in charge. "No problem," she added in English, "you can stay to rest." Max, exhausted, nearly kissed her. O'Leary, in his short pants and Harris tweed overcoat, did.

Sleeping arrangements were designed to maximize space utilization. Bodies on the floor alternated head to foot. Experienced groups knew enough to alternate positions so

53

that friends could communicate over the feet of strangers, who in turn communicated over the feet of strangers to them. Every square centimeter of space was occupied—the red-cheeked soup-makers even straddled bodies prone beneath the kettles.

A "wake-up" call was scheduled for 4:00 A.M.—ample time for more soup and a sunrise conquest of the summit. Conversation slowly died. Max nestled snugly against a steel beam near the entrance, and went to sleep. The labor pains did not begin until 1:30.

Why a pregnant woman in the last quarter of gestation would even *consider* climbing a mountain is the subject of another essay. It may have been like the stories one reads about women giving birth not realizing they were even pregnant. ("Woman Bears Twins at Half time of Bears Game—She and Husband Astonished.")

In any event, Mrs. Hiroshi Kanamori, 37, of Kanazawa, Ishikawa Prefecture, broke water. She was on her way.

Max later tried to reconstruct the exact sequence of events, but much was lost in the blur of sound, motion, and confusion resulting from 200 people suddenly awakening in the dead of night on the side of a mountain.

Max's first focused impression was that a lady was "in trouble" medically, but that people were shying away from her as if she were possessed. The lady was moaning and rolling from side to side, and her immediate neighbors on the floor were bumping, banging, and crawling out of the way. Since there really was no place to go, many folks ended up on top of each other.

Max recognized several words in the sudden babble of vocal sounds. One word, *sensei* (meaning among other things "doctor"), predominated. Max remembers shouting to O'Leary (whose head was at Max's feet) to get Dr. Meyer involved.

54

O'Leary, with the crisp precision of a sleepwalker, "baby-talked" his brother-in-law into the center of the arena. The lady, who had pulled down her trousers, squatted on her haunches and raised her face to the beams and planks forming the primitive roofing. (Max, still not completely awake, remembers looking up to see what she was looking at.) The cords and artery in the lady's neck stuck out—her face reddened. Dr. Meyer put his arm on her shoulder and with the other hand rubbed her heaving stomach. Pink strings and fluffy balls swayed with his motions.

After a few moments—which could have been 20 or 25 minutes as far as Max could recall—the lady shuddered and rolled on to her back. With her knees in the air, she delivered a bouncing baby daughter into the hands of Dr. Horst Meyer. He laid the infant on her mother's breast—a soup-lady cut the umbilical cord. The beauty of the moment—the magic of life aborning—will stay with Max to the grave.

The child was eventually named Hoko, incorporating the first two letters of Dr. Meyer's first name. The child's father, who had conveniently remained in the background during the adventure, hugged Horst Meyer with tears streaming down his weather-beaten face. There was no sleeping the rest of the night. Max, O'Leary, Miyabe, and especially Dr. Meyer, were celebrities in the little hut on the side of Mt. Fuji.

The climb to the summit was by comparison mundane. Max's group, seriously hung over from the 3:00 A.M. celebration, saw the sun rise. It was anticlimactic.

That happens every day.

What was amazing—what speaks tomes for word-of-mouth communication—was the extent to which Dr. Meyer's exploits had spread amongst the natives on the peak.

Max and his group were "congratulated" by perhaps as many as a thousand people on their descent in the morning sunlight. (Miyabe would give each cluster of folks a lusty *"sayonara"* as they slid down the mountain.) Ski outfit, duck-hunting costume, tennis shorts and overcoat, plus the beautiful Gloria's pink sweater, were easy to spot. People not only stared in wonder—they bowed!

It was during the taxi ride to Azabu that Max asked the question. It was occasioned by the nagging recollection of Dr. Meyer rubbing the lady's heaving stomach.

"What kind of doctor is Meyer?" repeated O'Leary, looking out the cab's window.

Meyer, speaking *no* English, stared straight ahead.

"Meyer," answered O'Leary, "is an economist."

Author's Note: Hoko Kanamori, six years old in 1987, thrives in a family with three older siblings. Her mother sends Max flowers each July 13.

Gloria's Day

THE INITIAL ADJUSTMENT to life in Japan is more difficult, by a long shot, for wives than any other member of a foreign family.

Husbands have jobs, profit and loss statements, employees, head office interference, and administrative guidance.

Children have algebra lessons, sports teams, and acne.

New wives, however, have nothing but long periods of

daily isolation, with meaningful communication limited to meat dialogue at the butcher's counter of the National Azabu Supermaket.

"Hello, one pound of ground beef, please."

"We have no pound of ground beef. Only gram."

"Of course, er, give me the same as one pound of ground beef—in grams."

"Half of kilogram is more than one pound of ground beef."

"I can well imagine. How much more?"

"Maybe—*sukoshi.*"

"Yes, maybe *sukoshi.* Well, give me one half-kilogram of ground beef," says the American housewife, hoping the butcher does not produce it in a wheelbarrow.

There are other opportunities for meaningful communication. The new-to-Japan wife must struggle with workmen over refinements necessary in the family abode.

"The doorbell does not work."

"Always have problems with flashing toilet."

"Not the toilet—the doorbell."

"Hai, water on the floor."

"No, the doorbell. It makes no sound. It does not go bing bong."

"Ping pong in toilet is problem."

The subsequent eruption in the guest bathroom confirms the building superintendant's observations. Unfortunately, requested emergency repairs are delayed by the absence of any signal on the doorbell that the plumber has arrived.

But the beautiful Gloria Danger, mother of three and new PTA member at three different schools, coped.

"I forgot to mention," stated Max at breakfast, "we're going to dinner tonight with a Valued Client."

"Why don't you go alone," said Gloria. "Those people never bring their wives."

"This one will. He was once stationed in New York," replied Max, "and he allowed his wife to visit him there—twice."

"Where and what time?" asked Gloria, already going through the mental checklist of arrangements that must be made in order to feed the children dinner and prevent fratricide during parental absence.

"The American Club at 6:30," said Max, grabbing his briefcase and heading for the front door. "I'll make all the arrangements."

That means, thought Gloria to herself after Max's departure, he may or may not remember to tell his secretary to phone for reservations.

10:00 Gloria learns that the Filipina maid, a regular Monday, Wednesday, Friday visitor who could sometimes be convinced to stay at night and babysit, was indisposed by hysteria brought about by family problems back home. Her father, six brothers, seventeen cousins, and one fiancé had all been arrested for defacing campaign posters.

10:36 The youngest Danger offspring unexpectedly returns home from school with the comment that all the teachers are too fussy. What's wrong with climbing from the tree in the playground to the roof of the classroom building?

10:37 A phone conversation with the school establishes the parent-teacher conference at 4:00 P.M.

11:15 The part-time job interview at Inter-dynamic Wonder Time Agency in Akasaka—advertised in capital letters in the *Japan Times*—reveals responsibilities somewhat more specific than "English-speaking foreigner desired for client interaction." The "five hours per day" began at 8:00 P.M. Masks were optional.

12:45 The Women's Group New Members luncheon at the Tokyo American Club really does start at 12:30. Gloria sat a block-and-a-half away from the speaker's table. The lady on her left, who had arrived in Japan the day before, wept throughout the meal.

2:45 The woman across the hall from the Danger apartment in Homat Cornucopia, a woman with four potential babysitting daughters between the ages of 15 and 18, confesses that the entire brood has been grounded. Offenses, said the woman, ranged from truancy to tattoos to not being home at all since last Thursday.

3:00 The meeting with the Valued Client, according to a phone call from Max's secretary, has been moved up to 6:00.

3:25 Gloria's regular hairdresser, Mr. Taki, goes on sick leave midway through the perm. Hemorrhoids, it is whispered.

4:00 The parent-teacher conference at the youngest Danger's school reveals that climbing from a tree in the playground to the roof of the classroom building involves a leap of some seven or eight feet—three stories above ground.

4:45 The piano teacher arrives. Unfortunately, the student, the Danger middle child, is at the dentist's office in Shibuya. Gloria takes the lesson instead and strikes a deal with the teacher to babysit that evening for ¥2,500 per hour.

5:30 Gloria discovers that the yakitori man in the Juban— the proposed source of the kids' dinner—is closed.

5:40 Gloria discovers that the piano teacher has never opened a can of soup before. The process is explained, and the art of putting butter on bread is demonstrated.

59

6:00 Gloria arrives at the American Club.

6:35 Max and the Valued Client, minus the Valued Client's wife, who had been hospitalized suddenly with a cold, arrive at TAC.

"How was your day, honey?" Max asks after the introductions.

"Oh, okay. I'll tell you about it later."

Gloria did. From 10:45 to midnight.

How to Japan

BOOKS ABOUND advising us on how to survive and flourish in an increasingly complicated world.

The *New York Times,* which for decades published the Best Sellers list in two categories, Fiction and Non-fiction, has had to add a third category—Advice, How-to and Miscellaneous. The action was prompted by the fact that the How-to books—ranging in scope from the mysteries of marital joy to the mechanics of Chinese cookery—were crowding everything else off the Non-fiction lists.

Inevitably, the How-to literary industry has zeroed in on Japan. The books are easy to spot at a distance—the covers for some reason are either red or yellow, and they usually feature a rising sun, a rendering of Mt. Fuji, a geisha, or a spectacular combination of all three.

We are treated, in these works, to sophisticated analyses of things Japanese. Because statistics are readily available on life in Dai Nippon, these books contain marvelous charts and priceless bits of information. ("The Ministry of Health reports that 67.5 percent of the population is always happy between 6:00 and 9:00 P.M., except Tuesdays.")

Motives within motives (within motives) are explored. Theories are presented. Conclusions are drawn. (A personal favorite is the Oriental rice culture versus the Western hunter/gatherer explanation of behavioral patterns. It's so neat.)

Similes are particularly creative. "Understanding Japan is like peeling an onion. When one layer is finished, there is a similar but different layer beneath." Tears aren't mentioned, but someday someone will work that in.

Max Danger, Expat, suggests that we may be getting ahead of ourselves, however. There are some very basic points about life in Japan which must be covered first.

As a community service, Max presents the following. Scholars frequently miss these things, and God knows expats need all the help they can get.

How to recognize "no" when you hear it:
1. The Japanese word for "maybe."
2. The Japanese phrase for "we understand."
How to recognize "yes" when you hear it:
1. The Japanese word for "maybe."
2. The Japanese phrase for "we understand."
How to get home from the Ginza at 11:30 P.M.:
1. Walk.
2. Wait until 1:30 A.M. and take a taxi.
How to lead the Head Office into thinking your Japan tour is reaching its conclusion:
Begin answering their telexes in Japanese.
How to demonstrate to the Head Office that your Japan tour should be extended:

Begin referring to the guys at MITI as Chuck, Ted, and Mike-san.

How to make a positive impression on your Japanese employees:

Call in sick several times a month.

How to make a negative impression on your Japanese employees:

Never get sick and stay in the office until they all go home.

How to make a positive impression on your Japanese neighbors:

Make a lot of noise, preferably mixed with choruses of "I Did It My Way," when you arrive home after midnight.

How to spend time with your teenage children:

Go out drinking with the staff after work and show up with a bunch of girls named Yuki at a Roppongi disco.

How to avoid being invited to employee weddings:

Rent a weekend beach house in Kamakura for $2,000 a month and let it be known you always go there.

How to avoid spending $2,000 a month for a weekend beachhouse in Kamakura:

Fly to Guam—it's cheaper.

How to recognize a car belonging to a foreigner:

1. No doilies on the seats.
2. No tissue box on the back shelf.
3. No danglies on the rear view mirror.
4. No Disneyland bumper stickers.
5. No huggable stuffed animals on the dashboard.
6. No polish on the exterior.

How to tell a fashionable male Japanese college student from a fashionable female Japanese college student from the rear:

You can't. (In fact, being in front doesn't always help.)

How to spend a quiet Sunday dozing in a comfortable chair:
Get into your car and enter any expressway.

How to throw bar hostesses off your trail:
Use only the business cards of new acquaintances which you'd otherwise just file.

How to file business cards of new acquaintances:
Pile them neatly in the upper left corner of your desk drawer until the pile tips over. Then throw them away.

How to eat Natto:
Don't.

How to frame a time reference for actions involving Japanese courts of law:
Think of your future grandchildren and their descendants.

How to guess the age of a Japanese individual:
1. If you think the person is 20, add five.
2. If you think the person is 30, add ten.
3. If you think the person is 40, add fifteen.
4. If you think the person is 50, add twenty.
5. There are no 60 year-olds in Japan—they're either 59 or 89.

How to distinguish a drinker from a genuinely embarrassed individual:
The drinker blushes and the embarrassed individual laughs.

How to confuse a cab driver:
Give directions to him in Japanese.

How to impress a Head Office Visitor:
1. Never use a company car. Explain that Otemachi and Azabu are hours apart on surface routes. Try to make the subway trips during rush hour.
2. Make certain the waiter at Tour D'Argent gives the Visitor the menu with prices during the little "snack after work."

3. Convert all American Club prices into U.S. dollars for the benefit of your Visitor.
4. Tell the Visitor you took three days off once last year in order to play one round of golf.
5. Throw your head back and laugh—let it loose—when he suggests a game of tennis.
6. Explain that there are thirteen ways to count from one to ten in Japanese.
7. Pray for a moderate earthquake (4.0 on the Richter scale, and whatever the hell it is on the Japanese scale).

How to deal with your situation in the Land of the Rising Sun:

Thank whomever you thank that you're not in Cleveland.

The Hospital Caper, Part I

THE ACHE, which for the past hour ebbed and flowed at regular intervals, was becoming constant. In fact, it was now being interrupted by sharp, white-hot stabs of excruciating pain. The pain was the type that accelerates to the threshold of endurance, lingers, then accelerates again to new levels of intensity that make previous agony mild by comparison.

Max Danger, Expat, could not believe it. He had never experienced anything like it in his life. He was genuinely terrified. Sitting alone in the back of a lurching taxi—on an evening rush hour odyssey from Ikebukuro to Azabu—Max actually began to pray. A flaming sword was being twisted around in his entrails. He couldn't breathe. His last conscious act, before his insides exploded, was reaching forward and grabbing the shoulders of a very surprised cab driver.

"Danger-san, *taka baka* mumble mumble *sawa huka* mumble, *desu ka?*"

"Er?"

"Taka baka mumble mumble *sawa huka* mumble, *desu ka?*"

"I don't know," Max said after a pause.

"Okay," said the nurse, turning and leaving the room.

Nurse? What the hell happened? Max hadn't the strength to call her back. A tube up his nose made an echoing hiss that seemed to surround his brain. Another tube was stuck into his arm. It was connected to a bottle of urine-colored fluid suspended above his head. A third tube, apparently attached to the middle of his torso, snaked from the blankets and disappeared under the bed. It's just like the movies, thought Max.

The wall opposite the bed had been splattered with some liquid that left brownish stains. Blood? Max felt giddy. What on earth had happened? The stains on the wall began to move and dance about. Pondering his sanity, Max fell asleep. He dreamt that he was being run over by a fourteen-wheel semi-trailer truck. With snow tires. Studded.

"You alive!" stated the man Max eventually came to know as Mr. Kubo, janitor and general maintenance supervisor at the Red Cross Hospital in Hiroo.

"But also very lucky," continued Mr. Kubo. He was translating the various remarks being made in the room by two doctors, a young nurse, and a matronly lady who fiddled with Max's tubes. Mr. Kubo had the ability to concentrate long paragraphs of conversation into succinct little phrases.

"Operation on you. They took away appendix."

"Good," said Max, still foggy from the semi-trailer truck dream.

"Appendix was broken and now you full of poison," continued Mr. Kubo. He also had the ability to deliver his translations without censoring their content. Since no one but Max understood what he was saying, no one stopped him.

"Short doctor here thinks you probably still die," said Mr. Kubo. "This nurse told other nurses outside you hairy."

"Oh?"

"Other doctor thinks you maybe not die."

"Good."

"But," concluded Mr. Kubo with Oriental wisdom, "he is younger."

Max was hospitalized for three months. The quick reactions of a Tokyo cab driver, and the obvious success of emergency surgery within minutes of his arrival at the hospital, had saved his life. The convalescence, during which gallons of antibiotics were pumped through his system, was tedious but not uncomfortable.

Mr. Kubo, deemed by the staff to have superior English language abilities, was summoned from his janitorial chores for any and all medical conferences in which Max was involved. ("When nurse asks how many toilets since yesterday, always say big toilet number and small toilet number separately.")

Gloria visited Max every day. The children visited on Sunday afternoons. Many of Max's business colleagues made the trip to his bedside more than once. Personal and business affairs were coordinated and handled for him by loved ones and friends. All major crises were averted.

But living in a Japanese hospital for three months exposes one to innumerable minor events that, if one is not careful, can consume one. Every day for Max was an adventure.

The first minor event, for example, became part of the permanent lore of the Red Cross tenth floor, west wing denizens. For weeks after, hospital staffers from other floors and other wings would visit Max's territory just to see the central character in the drama. It involved one of the first Japanese medical words Max learned, *"kensa,"* meaning "test."

Each day for about a week, after Max was allowed out of bed, a nurse would show up at precisely 2:00 P.M. It was nap time—curtains were pulled around beds, doors were shut, and all sound was reduced to a minimum. The nurse would whisper something unintelligible to Max. Her sentence always ended with the word *"kensa."* Consultation with Mr. Kubo revealed that a test of some sort was scheduled, and Max was to follow the nurse.

Max looked forward to these daily junkets which invariably had a nurse leading him to a new laboratory somewhere in the building for X-rays, blood tests, or other exotic examinations. Some nurses were friendly en route and basic communication could be established. Other nurses were all business.

On the day in question, a rather prim and humorless lady of reasonably attractive bearing said the magic sentence ending in the word *"kensa."* She turned and left the room. Max rolled into a sitting position on the edge of the bed, found his slippers, and began the flip-flop progress down the long corridor after the nurse.

Struggling to catch her, but mindful of the ban on noise during nap time, Max reflected upon the injustice involved in cold and aloof personalities contained in the bodies of some attractive women.

The nurse turned right at the junction of the main corridor. When Max arrived at the junction, he turned right, thinking that the fat little nurse who laughed and joked and served his breakfast each day would give a year's pay to be housed in the aloof one's body.

The nurse turned left down a narrow corridor. Max was particularly quiet as the progress took them near more be-curtained beds. The nurse turned right quickly, and by the time Max reached the corner, the door the nurse had entered was swinging shut.

It took several hours, with the help of Mr. Kubo, of course, to sort out and explain what happened—and why. Dozens of patients and staffers were interested. Essentially, the word *"kensa"* had *not* been used in the magic sentence. One word in English was used, however. The word was "cancelled." There was to be no test that day.

Max's arrival at the room that the nurse had entered came as a complete surprise—to both the nurse and to Max. She was just becoming comfortably seated as Max breezed in. Her screams rang out with astonishing volume. They were in the nurses' toilet.

The Hospital Caper, Part II

MAX HAD ALWAYS contended that the greatest experiments in history were not in the areas of science, technology or social organization. They were, instead, in the area of putting things in the mouth, chewing, and swallowing.

Clearly, one of the bravest humans ever to live was the first guy who, to what must have been the absolute astonishment of his pals in the cave, strolled over to the big-four-legged-hairy-thing-that-eats-grass, squeezed the tubes attached to the bag dangling between its hind legs, and *drank* what came out! His genius was probably not even recognized at first.

Or consider the gentleman who, probably on a dare, swallowed the insides of the hard, round, white thing that emerges from the rear end of the little-feather-creature-that-flies-and-goes-cluck. ("Hey, you guys. Let's try scrambling this stuff on a hot rock, and then we'll put it in our mouths.") Max dared not think about the initial man to eye speculatively the little oink-doggy-with-curly-tail-and-no-hair. It must have been gruesome at first.

But Max Danger, Expat, was faced with duplicating these feats of human bravery each day for three months at the Red Cross Hospital in Hiroo. Particularly at breakfast.

"Fish bery good for you," stated Miss Ohyama, breakfast nurse and sumo look-alike.

"I know," replied Max. "But this one's moving."

"I know," repeated Miss Ohyama. "That means it's fresh."

"I know," concluded Max, "and that's why I'm not eating it."

Patient and nurse stared at each other, neither articulating properly. Max wondered what Miss Ohyama would do if the fish, now scraping and scratching on the plate, flopped off the tray and into his lap.

"I'll get other fish," announced Miss Ohyama. She returned with a withered black creature with yellow eyes, no doubt highly salted.

"There," she announced. "This one *not* fresh."

Max never seemed to win these little exercises in logic with Miss Ohyama. The only solution to these encounters, a solution Max hit upon early in his convalescence, was to do something that in reality is rather shameful. He began to find ways of hiding portions of his unfinished meals.

It's not as easy as you might think to hide uneaten bits of food in a standard hospital room. A lot of people go in and out each day—after all it is *their* hospital. It wouldn't do to have the head nurse find fish buried amid the surgical bandages in the little cupboard next to the bed. Nor could one effectively stash the steamed mountain weeds in the pillowcase. Not only was the bedding changed every other day, but the soy sauce seeped.

The waste basket, of course, served in a pinch. The problem, however, was that the basket was always emptied before breakfast. That meant that nearly 24 hours would elapse before today's breakfast would be "picked up." It caused doctors and nurses, Max noticed, to twitch their noses suspiciously during evening examinations.

The toilet had been the obvious solution until the Sea Slug Stew Episode. Sea slug stew was served on Mondays, Wednesdays, and Saturdays. It consisted of dark, cylindrical, thumb-sized objects with the consistency of bubble gum. Grey round disks with large holes kept the dark objects company. Festooned on and about the surface were enormous carrot slices that resembled the cross-sections of redwood trees. Man-sized chunks of sweet potatoes hovered near the bottom, on top of several dozen kernels of corn.

The liquid in which the above delectables resided approached the consistency of paste as it cooled. The spoon would make popping noises as it stirred. In the liquid, and entwining the solid objects in the stew, was the type of blue-green weed that tangles outboard motor propellers in a lake. Max couldn't handle it.

He disposed of the first batch by waiting for it to cool, and then putting it in a paper bag. He convinced the beautiful Gloria to take it home and keep it in the refrigerator.

The second batch he dumped into his toilet. Max's toilet

70

door was visible the length of the hallway. At the entrance to his room, the toilet cubicle was designed so that T.V. cameras in the hall could transmit to monitors at the nursing station the comings and goings of the patients. If a door stayed shut too long, the nurses would know that there may be problems. Good system.

Max carved and scraped the stew into the toilet. He flushed. The toilet, apparently not accustomed to the load, backed up. With a vengeance.

Owing to a slant in the floor, the majority of the effluence rolled down the hallway, sea slugs, carrots, and corn merrily skipping and dancing on the tide. The sweet potatoes moved lethargically. The weeds became immediately entangled in wheelchairs, walkers, canes, and other machinery.

As Max emerged from the cubicle, for reasons he could not explain later, he waved at the camera. Then he sat on the chair in his room. The mess was cleaned up within a half-hour, but not before the doctors appeared on their morning rounds.

The upshot of the event was that Max couldn't quite bring himself to the point of admitting that he was throwing away food. It was not something to be proud of.

Instead, the doctors came to an unspeakable conclusion about the quality of Max's digestive system. He was put on rice and tea for the next eight meals. He now had the special digestion medicine to hide each meal.

Some stories have a happy ending. This one, about food in a Japanese hospital, does. One morning, a few days later, one of the other patients on the floor timidly entered Max's room as Miss Ohyama was leaving. Without saying a word, he picked up the bowl of stew and dumped it into a plastic bag he was carrying. He stuffed the bag into the folds of his *yukata*. He motioned Max to follow him.

They went down to the visitors' area on the lobby floor—

71

the man deftly dumping the plastic bag in a garbage container near the main entrance. They went to a small room, a cubby hole more accurately, behind the coffee machines. Inside were about a dozen guys Max recognized from his floor.

They each grunted *"ohayo."* They asked Max to join them. They were eating. From that morning, and for the next two-and-a-half months of his stay, Max's breakfasts were either McDonald's hamburgers, Kentucky Fried Chicken, Dunkin' Donuts, Shakey's Pizzas, or any similar commodity that "the regulars" could convince local shopkeepers to deliver to the cubby hole. Max had never had such a wonderful time.

The Hospital Caper, Part III

MAX DANGER, Expat, was released from the Red Cross Hospital in Hiroo three months to the day after his admittance. The doctors had said at the beginning that treatment to rid his body of the evil poisons spread by a burst appendix would take three months—and three months it took. A cynic might suggest that medical treatment in Japan is geared to coincide with initial prognoses, but the point is difficult to prove. At about the halfway mark in the episode, Max began to wonder what the authorities would do if he died. Probably, he figured, keep him on ice for another month-and-a-half to save faces.

For whatever reason, Max was discharged on a day deemed to be "lucky" according to the Japanese calendar.

(Being "unlucky," reflected Max, would probably mean he'd grow a new appendix, which in turn would rupture and start the process over again.) He was, in the words of his attending physician, "returned to healthy." He was also, in the opinion of friends, relatives and neighbors, returning from vacation.

But he had learned a lot. Stripped of pin-striped suits, Hanae Mori originals, and Gucci accessories, his 24-hour companions were concerned with the very real basics of existence. Certain values, aspirations, doubts, and fears are universal. Continuing to breathe is one.

Other values reflect cultural overlays and life-long conditioning. One gentleman, an 86-year-old architect with inoperable cancer, served as Max's bridge partner for several weeks. He would apologize profusely whenever the gruesome treatment he underwent interfered with "the game." The night he died—3:15 in the morning, actually—he told the nurse to apologize to his *gaijin* partner. The remaining players in the bridge group never got together again. The "group," as an entity, was gone.

A great deal has been written about medical treatment in Japan, and Max has read most of it. Quality of care and technological facilities are discussed, and the precautions that foreigners should consider are deftly explained.

But Max, from flat on his back in room 1002, developed a perspective from what could be best described as a "hands on" experience.

1. Japanese doctors never tell Japanese patients what's wrong with them. And patients never ask. One of Max's fellow patient-companions was a chap from the Foreign Ministry. He had been in the hospital at least a month longer than Max. He was well-educated and well-traveled. He had once been stationed in Washington D.C. Max

73

asked him what was wrong with him. "Lungs," came the reply. "Yeah, but what's *wrong* with them?" asked Max. The Foreign Ministry man hadn't the slightest idea. He had not even considered asking the doctor.

2. Hospital hygiene in Japan approximates that of the Shinjuku subway station. Subway stations in Japan are probably cleaner than any others on earth, but they're still subway stations. Visiting Hours would bring hordes of folk to the hospital—some to visit friends, some to get in from the rain. Max never saw a doctor or nurse wearing a little gauze face mask. Meanwhile, one out of 14 visitors wore face masks—the anticipated direction of germs was never clear. Keep in mind that many restaurants and lawyers' offices ask people to remove their shoes—hospitals do not. The ashtrays near the elevators were overflowing by the end of the day.

3. Nurses, with a considerably lower status in Japan than their counterparts elsewhere, nevertheless handle patients better than their male colleagues, the doctors. Max was given three intravenous bottles of antibiotics per day. Nurses in Japan are not allowed to stick needles into veins. Doctors must do it. In at least two out of three instances, the nurses would return after the doctors did their magic and re-insert the needle into a vein—the doctors having missed the target by as much as two centimeters.

4. Shaving abdominal and pubic hair is a universal tactic whenever surgical operations involve the lower stomach. Shaving abdominal and pubic hair is an every fifth day event in Japan—three months after the operation. It was at first an ordeal, it then became mildly sensual, but after several weeks it was again an ordeal. Max was never sure of the rationale behind the exercise, other than the possibility that it gave student nurses practical expe-

74

rience. Max would lie back, hands behind his head, stare at the ceiling and marvel at the circumstances that put him into a system whereby regular nurses were not allowed to stick needles into a vein, but giggling *student* nurses were encouraged to wield six-inch straight razors around areas of the body not normally exposed to sunlight. A great deal of tension was involved, particularly on Max's side.

5. The Far East Network—"a facility of the Armed Forces Radio and Televison Service"—to which Max was a 24-hour tunee, broadcasts in total an incredible amount of awful noise. Acid rock at 6:30 in the morning, introduced by Ma and Pa Kettle sound-alikes.

6. Japanese doctors, not accustomed to telling Japanese patients anything, tell foreigners everything. As a result of tests apparently apropos Max's diseased appendix, he was informed that he was near-sighted. He was advised not to drive until he got glasses.

7. Pornography, both soft and hard core, delivered by well-meaning friends and business associates, does not help.

8. Bathing, a national pastime in Japan, is not at first easy in a hospital. Admittedly, language difficulties contributed to the problem. Each morning the schedule of bath times was announced on the public address system: coordinating the ablutions of seventy patients in one bath for the wing required a certain amount of organization. Max, of course, had no idea what the voice in the sky was saying, and it wasn't until the middle of his third week that a student nurse, assigned to the abdominal and pubic hair detail, asked him about his bathing schedule. Max's answer—that he didn't even know where the bath was—brought immediate results. He even received a visit from the hospital's chief administrator, and his bedding was changed twice that same day. Still,

the normal bath schedule, which for Max was between 4:00 and 4:15 P.M. on Tuesdays and Saturdays, left something to be desired. Visiting Hour visitors would wipe out at least one of the sessions each week, and the resulting total of nine baths in twelve weeks would fall below, in Max's opinion, the national average in the darkest regions of the Amazon.

9. The Japanese sense of humor leans toward word-play, puns, and double entendres. (*"Shikimo"* means "color-blind," *"shikima"* means "horny." Try mixing those up in a sentence with the next lady who wants to know if you like her dress, and there'll certainly be a reaction.) Max's attempt at Western humor fell flat. When informed by the doctors—through the good services of Mr. Kubo, English-speaking janitor and translator—that massive doses of antibiotics might impair hearing, Max replied, "What?" He was thereafter sent for daily ear tests, even though he could still hear a hypodermic needle falling twelve rooms away.

Yet through it all, Max began gradually to appreciate what it must feel like to be Japanese. Hospitals, like prisons, epitomize structured institutional organizations. Japan epitomizes structured social organization.

At first the idea of being in a double-structured situation might appear to offer nothing but repression. But who organizes better than the Japanese? Mustn't they have the ability to accommodate individual instincts within the structures? Doesn't this place seem to work?

Once Max got the hang of it, once he realized where the boundaries were, the freedom within the parameters was almost total. The key is for the components of a group to make their own adjustments to each other within the boundaries of rules and regulations. Once that is done, behavior by the components is then regulated by the group—not the rules. The group, in a hospital, includes doctors, nurses, administrators, patients, and the English-speaking janitor—all interacting.

Max knew that the authorities realized he and a dozen other guys slipped out each morning for breakfasts of junk food. Gradually, the normal hospital breakfast of quivering fish and sea slug stew was replaced by fresh fruit and juices—an attempt to keep their preferred diet balanced.

Max was allowed to go home every now and then during his hospital confinement. In fact, one of the doctors drove him over to Homat Cornucopia on Christmas Eve (a time everyone figured must be important to a *gaijin*). The excursions were never recorded nor remarked upon.

Max had a visitor one evening—a college classmate on a business trip to Japan—who arrived at the hospital long after Visiting Hours had ended. They sat up playing gin rummy until 3:00 A.M.—in the nurses' lounge.

Max's next door neighbor, a bicycle freak, kept his machine in Max's room. He would come in each night after "lights out," and while *his* roommate played mah jong with an old man in a wheelchair, Max's neighbor would tinker with his gears on Max's floor. Max, meanwhile, read novels and learned the words for "the goddam chain won't go on the goddam sprocket" in Japanese.

Max's middle child, interested in nursing, but at eleven forbidden by rules to be in the hospital at all, frequently helped serve dinner to all the patients in the wing.

And as for baths, once it was clear that Visiting Hours conflicted with Max's time on the schedule, adjustments were allowed. From the third week on, he bathed every single evening from 11:00 to midnight. No other component in the group was bothered by it, and things were slow at that time of night anyway. He had, more often than not, help scrubbing his back from the student nurse brigade. Not bad.

Try doing any of that, concluded Max, in a less-structured society, where rules are Rules.

Memos for All Occasions

MAX DANGER, Expat, discovered early in the Tokyo assignment that written communication is absolutely necessary if any arrangement is to be irrevocably confirmed.

In the States, for example, it is entirely possible for two individuals to agree verbally on a course of action. ("Golf? Okay. Meet at the Club at nine.")

In Japan, the same exchange requires written confirmation—if for no other reason than to pass the inevitable map. ("To confirm our phone talk today golf play start is 9:00 A.M., and enclosed is map which shows either go by car or go by train but both ways is three hours unless stay overnight first at near town which is second map attached to picture of golf course.")

In addition to map passing, written communication completes files. And Japanese files must be complete. It is said that because all Japanese agreements were for centuries verbal—a man's word being his bond—the introduction of written documentation by Western devils threw the custom for a loop. Once things moved from the realm of trusting one's word, and all the non-verbal stomach-to stomach communication implicit in a deal, anything written must specifically spell out all the spoken and unspoken ramifications of an agreement.

Western auto insurance policies, for example, state that the company will pay in the event of a wreck. Japanese auto policies say the same thing, but they also describe what is meant by a wreck. ("Run into other car going same way, run into other car going opposite way, run into other car from side way, run off road into agricultural field, run off road into non-agricultural field, run into object not moving, run into standing person, etc., etc.") Running into, let's say, a space capsule which had somehow landed on the Shuto Expressway, would cause significant consternation in the Japanese underwriting bullpen. The claim would eventually be paid, but a great deal of wind-sucking would occur first, *and* an endorsement to the policy would have to be licensed in order to handle future contingencies of the same ilk. ("Space capsules, space vehicles, space junk, etc.")

Max, therefore, found that it was practical to have at his fingertips a package of memos and phrases which, if employed judiciously, covered most circumstances in which he was likely to be involved. The phrase "to confirm" appeared an inordinate amount of times, as did the phrase "we apologize."

TO A DISTRIBUTOR: "To confirm, we apologize that our paper-towel holders (baseball bats / surgical tape / cotton underwear / fruit-juice dispensers) did not have the prior approval of the Kitchen Safety Association (Japan Baseball Association / Medical Workers' Cooperative / Skin Protection Agency / Everybody Consumers' Union), and are therefore being held by the Customs authorities. We anticipate prompt resolution of the matter and the timely release of our products from government warehouses."

To a joint venture partner: "To confirm, we apologize that the Chairman of our corporation was not aware of the significance of Boys' Day (the Emperor's Birthday / Vernal Equinox / Respect for the Aged Day / Sports Day), and has planned his trip to Japan despite that gaffe. We anticipate your participation in the meetings scheduled during the holidays."

To the roppongi police station: "To confirm, I apologize for parking the car on Sunday night in a taxi zone in front of Antonio's (Emile's / Meidi-ya / Lo Heian / Chianti's / Tony Roma's), and I'll never do it again. The fact that taxis never appear in those spots at that time must have distorted my otherwise good judgement."

To the minato ward office: "To confirm, I apologize for not reporting on a timely basis my wife's (my sons' / my daughter's / my own) return to Japan from vacation. I assure you I tried, but taxis kept going to where you used to be, and to where you are returning, but not to where you actually are. May I complete future transactions at the Mori Building Headquarters?"

To the president of the tokyo american club: "To confirm, I apologize for my son falling asleep on the lobby floor (my other son skipping through the Main Dining Room in his swimming suit / my daughter doing back-flips from the life guard's chair / my wife driving the car over the feet of the parking lot attendant / my company's inability to process payments on a current basis), and I anticipate no further difficulties in this regard."

To the ministry of finance: "To confirm, I apologize for my Head Office's inexplicable transfer of U.S.$250,000 to our local account without reporting the transaction in the generally accepted manner. As I explained, an error in our New York Accounting Department apparently funded us in Japan instead of, ah, Jakarta."

TO A JAPANESE EMPLOYEE: "To confirm, I apologize for raising my voice (implying non-cooperation / questioning expenses / looking askance), and my apology is approved by the Employee's Union, the Section Chiefs' Council, and the Managing Directors' Arbitration Committee. Your kind return to the office, at your convenience, would be in the greater interest of the group as a whole. Your past contributions, and your future potential, make us partners in our quest for business excellence.

TO A GAIJIN EMPLOYEE: "Get back to work immediately you bloody damn idiot, or I'll kill your wife and eat your children."

The Hateful Bastard

AS A GENERAL rule, it is easier in life to be forgiven than to obtain permission. Corporate businessmen know this—entire careers have been built upon the principle. Wives know this—entire wardrobes have been assembled upon the principle. Children know this—their entire lives operate on the principle.

Another general rule, however, is that what works in life doesn't necessarily work the same way in Japan.

"Boy cannot come to Japan," announced the immigration official.

"But he's already here," explained Max Danger, Expat, pointing to the youngest of his three children.

"Sorry, boy cannot come."

Impasse. It was 11:51 P.M. at Narita International Airport. The Danger family had flown non-stop from New York. Home leave was over. School would start in a few days. The food on the plane had been awful. The movie, something about a girl who is really a bird (the kind that flies) and a guy who is really a wolf (the kind that eats grandmothers) had been pretty good the first four or five times, but the sixth showing, on the sixth and final leg of the journey, had broken the Danger family tolerance barrier. In short, everyone was in a perfectly rotten mood.

"But he's with us," reasoned the beautiful Gloria.

The immigration official ignored her.

"He's only five years old," she added.

The immigration official ignored her.

"We're Americans," she concluded.

The immgration official looked up at Max.

"Boy cannot come to Japan."

The Danger family had flown around the world, had toured in five countries, had crossed five national borders. Every single Japanese visa and re-entry permit was current. The problem was that the youngest Danger's U.S. passport had expired during the first week of the trip. Not an airlines official, border guard, or customs examiner anywhere had noticed it until the return "home" to Narita. And an expired passport invalidates visas and re-entry permits. The youngest Danger was now in a category below Cambodian refugees, assuming, in Japan, that's possible.

"Go out of line please! Wait for inspector," the official stated with finality.

The Danger family was given ample time to discuss the ramifications of the situation whilst waiting for the inspector. They had been shown to a room in the immigration area. There were several "customers" ahead of them.

One lady, with a shaved head and flowing pink robes, insisted that as a citizen of the world she did not require a passport from any one country. Another customer, a balding middle-aged gentleman of Middle Eastern appearance, whose shirt and trousers may have fit 15 kilos ago and whose sandals were held together with tape, explained that his passport was stolen on the plane. However, his explanation went, since he was going to be a student at Tokyo University he should be allowed to enter the country. No, he did not have correspondence from the University to show the inspector. The solution in both cases seemed to be overnight detention and an early flight out the next day.

Between recriminations and subdued bursts of passion within the Danger family, one factor emerged with crystal clarity. It was Max's fault.

"What are you going to tell them, Dad?" asked the youngest, with not a little concern.

"He's going to tell them that he's a bonehead," soothed the beautiful Gloria.

"Why don't you tell them," added his middle child, "that you know the President of the American Club?"

"I'm going to tell them the truth," said Max. "I'm going to tell them my secretary screwed up, or something."

"No," chimed in the eldest child, a budding comedian, "tell them that you're a citizen of the world *and* a student at Tokyo University."

The session with the inspector was predictable.

"Obviously there is a mistake," said Max.

"But expired passport is same as no passport," said the inspector.

"My embassy will issue a new passport for him tomorrow morning," said Max.

"But no visa to see Embassy," said the inspector.

The immigration official who first noticed the expired date wandered into the room. It's amazing, thought Max, how some bastards are immediately hateable. That twerp was actually sneering.

"*If* the passport had been valid," continued Max, turning his attention back to the inspector, "the Japanese documentation *would* be in order."

"Of course," confirmed the inspector. "Very easy."

"Now what?" asked Max.

The immigration official—the hateful bastard—walked over to the inspector. He said something to him in Japanese. Max realized that he was as close as he had ever been to jumping up and strangling another human being.

"Can you write apology letter?" asked the inspector.

"Now?"

"Now."

He did. It took four drafts for an acceptable combination of words to emerge to the satisfaction of the inspector. Max not only admitted full culpability, he promised that such deviant behavior would never, ever occur again. His children's children would not even do such a thing. The youngest Danger was admitted to Japan at 1:10 A.M.

It is easy to despise bureaucracy when one presents problems outside the norm. The intractability of Japanese bureaucrats, stated Max to the family as they roamed around the virtually deserted baggage area looking for their belongings, approaches madness. Max, in fact, repeated the theme several dozen times in several dozen different ways until they found where their bags were stored. More forms had to be completed, each with an implied apology for being late. The airport had shut down for the night.

Standing in front of the darkened terminal—not a cab, bus, or limousine in sight—was probably the low point of the evening. By now, Max had resolved to find that first immigration official someday, the hateful bastard who had noticed what no one else had noticed on their trip around the world, and commit acts of vengeance upon his body too crude for exposure in a family publication.

A lone car drove up and stopped.

"Want ride? I live on way past Azabu."

It was the hateful bastard. He drove them all the way to Homat Cornucopia. He helped carry the bags into the apartment. He even helped the youngest Danger, the sleepy illegal alien, up the steps. He stayed for a cup of tea. He left for home, someplace near Yokohama, at 4:30 A.M.

"You know," said Max to the beautiful Gloria as they finally lay in bed, "I'm glad we took the assignment in Tokyo."

The Japan We Know and Love

MAX DANGER, Expat, returned from his first Home Leave trip with the not very original observation that the real world understands very little of Japan. Particularly in America.

The good people of the United States *do* have a "feel" for other countries—a situation no doubt tied to early waves of immigration and assimilation.

Americans know that Brits, for example, have a Queen, more often than not have had a King, now have a Prince with a pretty wife, and it rains a lot in their country. It is understood that the folks in England think they know about wine, drink warm, bitter ale, and speak a peculiar form of English (caused, perhaps, by heartburn). Their culture is pervasive—fish, chips, darts, espionage novels, wrinkled club ties, and chartered accountants abound. Maggie and Ron relate—people in Kansas have heard of Shakespeare. Yes, Americans know England.

Americans also know Germany. People there have red cheeks, eat sausages, plan their fun carefully (and then, by God, have it), obey rules, wear leather shorts by choice, are precise in business, and are descended from men who fought on the Russian Front. Germany is located in the large land-mass on the other side of England. (The land-mass is called "Europe.")

Italians sing and make great spaghetti, have had 105 governments since 1945, live in palaces built in 1374, have contributed more than anyone to the "fine arts," and blow each other apart under the terms of secret "codes of honor." (Interestingly, an Italian is recognized as having "discovered" America, which is similar to saying Marco Polo "discovered" China.) Italy is attached to the bottom part of Europe.

The French, whose bread turns to stone overnight, speak in the language taught in U.S. high schools and colleges. (Except they don't. There is no record of any Frenchman ever understanding one word of U.S. high school/college French.) Americans accept, in fact, anticipate, the arrogance of a people addicted to snails, truffles (snorted out by pigs), fungi, and cream sauces poured over meat. Americans know that the French colony in heaven is surrounded by high walls—to maintain the illusion, for the French, that they are the only ones there. The French "discovered" Illinois.

Scandinavians went to Minnesota and found *Lake Woebegon*. The Irish embarked upon twin careers spawned by a common ancestor known as a "sub rosa enhancement"— i.e., politics and police work.

Spaniards take the form of Cubans and Mexicans—one driven by the poverty of dictatorship, the other by the poverty of democracy. Puerto Rico is the 51st State.

All Scots once upon a time wore skirts, but now wear blue jeans and dominate the Top Forty Country Music lists. (Bagpipes, whose melancholy whine was replaced by fiddles in America, were originally a sardonic gift from the Irish. The Scots, to everyone's surprise, took them seriously.)

Jews control show business, top-level finances, and jewelry—in other words, all the things that count. The American Indian was screwed by the white man, but boy could Jim Thorpe run. Chinese put out good food cheaper than McDonald's, starch collars, and had something to do with the railroads "out West." Polacks provide comic relief.

Black Americans who, with the original English, form the most central of fibers in the U.S. tapestry, brought to the States African tribal rituals and related nonsense which today is the basis of more cultural expression than many care to admit.

Yes, Americans have a handle on the peoples and the countries comprising and surrounding them.

But Japan?

The average American doesn't know enough about Japan even to form an outrageous stereotypical impression that is moderately close. (After all, a lot of Irishmen *are* policemen and politicians.)

The following snippets of conversation and disjointed phrases were faithfully recorded on napkins, the backs of envelopes, and American Express receipts by Max during his Home Leave trip:

87

Amtrack conductor on the Bronxville line to Max: "Have you heard of the speed-train they (the Japanese) have that goes non-stop from Tokyo to Hong Kong?"

Bloomingdales clerk to Max: "What's that?"
Max to clerk: "An international travellers' check issued by a Japanese bank."
Bloomingdale's clerk to Max: "Japanese don't have banks; they have to pay cash."

Car rental clerk (Williamsburg, Virginia) to Max: "What's that?"
Max to clerk: "A Japanese driver's license."
Car rental clerk to Max: "Gee, you look just like one of us."

Society Hostess (Washington D.C.) to Max at a party: "Other than a language variation, aren't the Japanese the same as Koreans?"

New York City cab driver to Max: "We should stop giving the bastards aid. After all, they started World War II."

Waldorf Astoria waiter to Max: "If I had it to do over again, I woulda moved to Japan years ago."
Max to waiter: "Why?"
Waiter to Max: "Them Japanese are the best tippers in the world."

Chicago policeman (confidentially) to Max: "You know the Japanese steal cars here, ship them back to China, copy them, and beat our brains out with the imitations."

A great aunt to Max: "My poor boy, you should arrange to get away from there (Japan) as soon as possible."
Max to great aunt: "Why?"

Great aunt to Max: "Children should not sleep on the floor."

Antique store proprietor in Cripple Creek, Colorado to Max: "I hear they eat raw meat there (Japan)."
Max to proprietor: "No, they eat raw fish."
Proprietor to Max: "Bullshit."

Denver advertising executive and former WWII Occupier to Max: "The broads were great. Do you know a girl there named Masuko?"
Max to Occupier: "Well, in fact, yes—"
Occupier to Max: "Tell her to send me a picture—to the office."

Asian Studies Professor at the University of Hawaii to Max: "The Japanese have the best educational system in the world."
Max to the Professor: "Well, a lot of it is based upon mere rote memorization—"
Professor to Max: "If that's the way you think, then you're the wrong man for the job in Japan."

The Affair, Part I

MAX, BY MOST community standards, was a straight arrow. Oh, there were occasional love trysts in Morocco and bouts of passion 'neath Polynesian palms, but these were imaginary adventures. In reality, Max was remarkably chaste.

The reasons for are as varied as the pressures against

sexual and emotional fidelity. It goes without saying that as a loving husband and caring father, Max never had any particular inclination to violate the marriage vows he had exchanged with the beautiful Gloria.

It could also be said that Max's awareness of the chaos often wrought by extramarital entanglements was a factor. His upstairs neighbor, for example, had been married four times, alimony payments were eating up his Cost of Living Allowance, a son by a former marriage had moved to Japan and was walking around Roppongi with pink and green hair, and his current wife had just left him—taking his Ray Charles tapes with her. To add to the quality of his life, his secretary was obviously pregnant. He may be having fun, thought Max, but he sure looked exhausted.

There was another reason, if the truth were known, for Max's fidelity. All his life Max had recognized opportunities in retrospection rather than anticipation—the classic "Oh, *that's* what she meant" syndrome. (Max's buxom secretary in the States had once asked him to her apartment to help fix her broken bed. Max declined, explaining that he was not good with a hammer.)

But something, maybe the Tokyo water, was getting to Max. Idle speculation about the charms of the opposite sex was becoming more frequent—and vivid. "There sure are a lot of young lovelies flouncing and giggling about. And my, oh my, what tidy little bodies." Unchecked, the theme gradually developed.

They seem so friendly, and anxious to please.

They range all the way from "cute" to sultry.

They appear to be undemanding.

They dress well and always look groomed.

They undress well, at the drop of a hat, in clubs and show bars.

They embody the Oriental mystique.

They look at me and blush.

They look at me and don't blush.

They look at me.

Yes, Max was approaching the "wonder what it's like" stage without actually realizing it. These things can happen, of course.

"You always so friendly," purred Miss Fujii. "I think you have good spirit."

"Well, I ah, er, of course, er, so do you," replied Max glibly.

"You must have many friends in Japan," continued Miss Fujii, counting Max's banknotes with the speed-of-light efficiency that is part of the bank tellers' standard training program.

"Oh, yes, er no, ah, it depends," quipped Max, never at loss for words.

"You spend all the money on weekend?" asked Miss Fujii, flashing her dark almond eyes at Max as she piled the cash on the plastic tray.

"Yes, the beautiful Glo—I mean, I'm going wind surfing."

"Oh, I love wind surfing," exclaimed Miss Fujii, enthralled, "you must be very good."

"Yes, heh, heh, it's easier than it looks," confirmed Max Danger, Expat.

Now, the fact that the closest Max had ever come, or ever wanted to come, to wind surfing was reading an article about it the night before in *Sports Illustrated* was not the point. Young Miss Fujii, one of the cutest bank tellers in creation, was vitally interested. Max had hit, so to speak, her hot button.

"See you Monday," declared Max, flashing a finger sign he had seen in Hawaii which meant something about big waves.

"I envy you," sighed Miss Fujii, catching Max's gaze in hers.

That was the beginning of what Max rationalized to himself as being an opportunity to indulge in speculation up close. Nothing evil intended, mind you, just a little more specific titillation.

The next in-depth conversation, two bank visits, and one week later, took place in a salaryman's lunch pit in the basement of a building across from Max's office. The lunch rush was over, and Max was dawdling over green tea when Miss Fujii walked in. It was not quite a coincidence.

"Oh, Mr. Danger, I never saw before you here."

"It's my first time," replied Max, normally a Press Club habitué, "but I noticed you going in here yesterday."

"I'm glad," said Miss Fujii sitting on a tiny stool opposite Max. "I'm embarrassed my legs," she added suddenly.

"Why?" asked Max, realizing he'd never seen or noticed her legs behind the bank counter.

"Not good to foreigner," she explained, looking down at them.

"They seem nice to me," said Max, also looking down at them. They were nice. Maybe her best feature, Max realized, but they were surprisingly hairy.

"Why don't Japanese girls sha— I mean, do you like your job at the bank?" asked Max, editing the question in mid-phrase.

"But good for wind surfing," replied Miss Fujii, still one thought behind.

The session continued for the duration of Miss Fujii's lunch break, with Max introducing subjects, any subjects, that would steer the conversation away from wind surfing. Max had re-read the *Sports Illustrated* article in an attempt to learn some of the buzz words, but he quickly assessed that Miss Fujii was way ahead of whoever wrote the article.

Only a consideration of her physical attributes seemed to hold her attention for any length of time.

"Well, I'm a foreigner, and I don't think your, ah, breasts look too small," said Max, in response to a question he had never been asked before. The drift of the conversation had become agreeably titillating, but Miss Fujii suddenly announced that she had to go back to work. She paid for her own lunch.

The stroll to the bank was unremarkable except for Max's last utterance.

"Let's have dinner sometime," he said, surprising himself. Max had not spoken that phrase to a female in almost twenty years.

"Tomorrow night okay?" asked Miss Fujii.

"Yes," replied Max.

They stood looking at each other in silence. Miss Fujii smiled. Max smiled. Miss Fujii demurely looked down at her feet—she was pigeon-toed, Max noticed.

"Let's meet at six o'clock in the Old Imperial Bar," suggested Max.

"Okay," said Miss Fujii.

She looked at Max for a moment longer, then turned and walked briskly into the bank.

"What on earth," Max asked himself on the way back to his office, "am I doing?"

The Affair, Part II

"HERMAN AND ETHEL Gunderson of Flat Fork, Nebraska are celebrating 72 years together on their way to forever," announced the beloved Paul Harvey on the morning news. "And Zsa Zsa's ninth marriage is reportedly in trouble."

"I wonder," asked Max of his reflection in the shaving mirror, "if Paul Harvey ever had an affair?"

"I'd give a million dollars and two of the three children," answered the reflection, "to prove it."

Max's morning routine seldom varied. He would awaken to the sports scores of games scheduled for broadcasting later in the day, shave to Paul Harvey, shower and dress during the Swap Shop ("1978 Bongo Van for $600 or best offer") interlude, and comb his hair with the 8:00 news. (Once, running late and still at the teeth brushing phase during the news, he nearly choked as the announcerette mispronounced three words in the same sentence—including the last name of the mayor of New York City.)

But this morning was a little different. He paid special attention to his grooming routine. Tonight would be the night—for reasons still undefined—that he would meet Miss Fujii for dinner.

Max had some second-hand knowledge of the ramifications of conducting affairs in Japan. One of his colleagues, a legend within the corporation, had become intimate with a Japanese clerk who worked, of all places, in the American

Embassy. They "broke up" one tearful night on the eve of the man's home leave trip to the States. The man, a summer bachelor, planned to spend a few weeks with his vacationing family prior to their return to Tokyo. The girl, quite lovely by all reports, took it badly. She direct-dialled, from his apartment, the phone number for Weather Information in New York. She left the phone off the hook. Max's colleague returned to Tokyo with his family to face a telephone bill representing 30,240 minutes of overseas tolls—a significant portion of his annual salary. The man had since been transferred to Nigeria.

Another acquaintance, a banker with impeccable credentials, had discovered too late that his compliant secretary hedged her bets. Their photographs, taken during a "business trip" to Bangkok, indicated a warm and affectionate relationship. The secretary had arranged for the development of the film. She had two prints of each photo made. When the banker with impeccable credentials changed his mind about things, the second set of prints ended up on his boss' desk in New York. His boss was also his father-in-law. The man was transferred to the banker's equivalent of Nigeria—the newly created Foreign Loan Department in Des Moines, Iowa.

But these awful things would not happen with the charming Miss Fujii. She was merely a wholesome girl with great, if slightly hairy, legs whose interests were simply "getting to know foreigner with good spirit."

Dressed for battle, Max bade the beautiful Gloria farewell, explaining that he'd be late due to a mumble mumble business dinner mumble. He admonished his youngest for throwing scrambled eggs at his oldest, stepped on the cat's tail, and strode into the morning sunshine filtering through the hallway *shoji* in the lobby of Homat Cornucopia. He was wearing his new Christmas underwear.

95

"I'm sorry so late," gasped Miss Fujii upon her entrance to the Old Imperial Bar. "We had union meeting after work."

"That's okay," said Max. He had more or less given up on Miss Fujii after 40 minutes of waiting, and was now into his third martini—a special consolation for jilted lovers.

"Had to run from taxi," she explained, settling into the chair opposite Max and crossing her legs.

"Would you care for something to drink?" asked Max. He fully expected a five minute display of indecision over the preferability of Campari and soda to orange juice.

"Bourbon," replied Miss Fujii instantly. "With just a splash."

Miss Fujii was becoming more attractive by the minute. Although agreeably slim, everything about her was round. No sharp angles, no unsightly bulges. Her skin was smooth and appeared tan. Her shoulder-length hair, parted in the middle, made an oval frame for a face that was both childishly cute and maturely beautiful. Depending upon angles and lights, she could be coy, she could be passionate. She was wearing a tissue thin, white sleeveless blouse which revealed a fuller figure than Max had noticed before.

"I take off my blouse," announced Miss Fujii after the drinks were served.

Two waiters rushed over to Max and pounded his back. When the coughing stopped, one of the waiters wiped up the remains of Max's drink. Through the tears in his eyes, Max saw Miss Fujii calmly remove the red union badge that had been pinned to her blouse.

"I always forget about this," she added, dropping the badge into her purse.

The misunderstanding set the tone for the evening. During Miss Fujii's second bourbon (and Max's fifth martini), she announced that she liked her job at the bank but she had "no chance to feel a man." Careful questioning revealed that she meant something about not having adult responsibilities.

Similarly, during dinner she stated: "My sex is exciting." Careful questioning again revealed that she meant something about females being too nervous.

In fact, it wasn't until the disco phase of the evening, when Miss Fujii whispered, "I like to warm bed," that Max gave up the careful questioning. Sure as hell it would mean something about the air conditioning system in the Lexington Queen, or skiing in Hokkaido. (An earlier discussion about Max's bed had to do with why the mattress wasn't hung out of the window each day.)

Things were going reasonably well on one plane—Max could well imagine physical compatibility, particularly during the slow dances. But anything beyond that would be a struggle.

Twenty-one musical groups had been mentioned during the course of the evening; Max recognized the names of two. Four automobile models were discussed; Max had not heard of any of them. Entire movie scenarios were analyzed; Max had only read *Time* magazine reviews. Sleeping out on Chiba beaches was extolled; Max could only visualize Coney Island.

To be fair, the problem was on both sides. Miss Fujii had never heard of a) the Chicago Cubs, b) the Platters, c) Bill Cosby, d) the Korean War, e) Staten Island, f) Leo Tolstoy, g) Herman Gunderson, Ethel Gunderson, Zsa Zsa Gabor or Paul Harvey. (She could probably pronounce Mayor Koch's name, however.) On any plane above the physical one, the deal was a bummer.

There are no clever endings to these kinds of stories. Miss Fujii turned out to be a nice kid. In a way, Max enjoyed being around an extremely attractive, probably sensuous, young woman. She looked good, smelled good, and felt good.

From her point of view, Max represented an intriguing wordliness, if only because he had lived in various places and didn't hang his mattress out of the window. He didn't lecture her, he only seemed to be interested in why she did things.

They said "good-night" outside the disco. Max walked home from Roppongi. He felt bad about what he did; he felt good about what he didn't do. He didn't sleep. His middle child, normally the healthiest of the lot, was up vomiting most of the night.

The Rules and the Dead Australian

Max occasionally lunched in a small restaurant near his office. The food was unremarkable and the decor decidedly spartan. Between noon and 1 o'clock it was jammed with salarymen and office ladies inhaling food on a non-stop basis. The place dispensed curried rice by the ton.

After 1 o'clock, when the hordes returned to their offices, the restaurant became a haven of tranquility for Max. On those rare days without a scheduled business luncheon, Max would select a corner table and leisurely apply himself to the little things that must be done, but for which there is never enough time.

It was there, balancing his checkbook, Max discovered that he and the beautiful Gloria had overdrawn their joint bank account to the tune of ¥131,465.

It was there, late one January, he finished addressing the Christmas cards Gloria had given him two months earlier.

It was there, over a period of several months, he learned all sixteen of the kanji he now recognized.

It was there, one hot afternoon, he first saw the Australian. Max noticed the Australian primarily because he was a *gaijin*. Until that day, Max had never seen another foreigner in the restaurant. Max also noticed that the Australian was the only male wearing a suit jacket—everyone else, including Max, was in shirt sleeves. A traveler, Max figured.

The Australian's voice boomed across the half empty restaurant as he negotiated a mundane business transaction with a Japanese man seated opposite him. Max listened for a few moments—less interested in the business deal than in the man's rich, colorful accent.

As was his custom, Max dawdled over his food. He would take a bite of his *sando,* read a few pages of *Time* magazine, then take another bite. His eating pace was certainly slower than anyone that restaurant's staff had ever seen before. With a pair of waiters hovering over him, Max was reminded of the two laboratory rabbits, caged and awaiting their place in the history of science, who were watching two laboratory humans making love on the floor. "I can't understand," said one rabbit to the other, "why they do it so slowly."

Max finished his meal and went to the cash register just as the Australian was walking out of the door. The Australian was a large man of about 55 who looked fit and the picture of health. He was probably a former lifeguard, Max surmised, and had rowed tiny boats over twenty foot waves for fun, or whatever similarly mad things those people down there seem to enjoy doing.

The Australian and his Japanese colleague had gone their separate ways by the time Max emerged from the restaurant.

The Australian's way was also Max's, and he followed the man at some distance down the narrow alley leading to the main street. The alley was reasonably well-traveled. A pretty girl, walking toward Max, pleasantly diverted his attention until she passed.

The Australian had already fallen to the pavement by the time Max looked his way again. He was lying across the alley and was thrashing about in obvious agony. Max ran up to him, but by the time he got there, the man had stopped thrashing. He was very still.

People have heart attacks anywhere, anytime. The reactions of those in the vicinity of an emergency run the gamut from indifference to total altruism. For every Kitty Genovese story in New York, there are countless other stories of strangers risking life and limb for their fellow man.

Max had always figured that he'd be one of the caring souls, but there was also the nagging thought in the back his mind that "becoming involved" was usually a problem. And messy.

Deliberation was not possible, however, as Max stood over a man turning blue on the ground. He began pounding on the chest of a complete stranger and alternately blowing air into the stranger's mouth and down into his lungs.

Because the thrashing had broken the crystal on the man's watch, thereby stopping the movement, Max was later able to calculate that he had kept at the routine for one hour and twelve minutes. During that time, the Australian seemed to revive twice. He made an attempt to get to his feet the second time. Max succeeded in keeping him still, but then realized that the stillness was due to the man's heart stopping again.

What else happened during the one hour-and-twelve-minute period? Returning to the scene several weeks later and counting the passers-by, Max figured that at the rate

100

of seven people a minute, 504 folks stepped over them as he and the Australian wrestled obscenely with death in the alley. Of that group one person, a *ramen* delivery boy, stopped and watched the two *gaijin* for a while. Between chest pounding and lung blowing, Max asked the kid to get help. He was probably the one who did call the ambulance, although it could have been any of the other 503 people passing the scene.

Are the citizens of Tokyo more, or less, callous than their counterparts elsewhere? Hard to say. Would people in Kansas City, for example, stop and help two Asians embracing on the ground—the active one periodically throwing up, the passive one having voided his kidneys and bowels on the pavement? Hard to say.

The ambulance people slapped a portable oxygen unit on to the Australian, but after a minute or two it became obvious that the man was already dead. Max watched them. In fact, now some of the passers-by stopped and watched also. Authority had arrived, so it was okay.

The police asked Max to go with them to their station to complete a "Witness of Death" report. The Australian—he with the formerly rich and colorful accent—was trundled off to wherever people who die on the streets of Chiyoda-ku go.

Max went with the police to their station. He answered their questions. He completed their forms. He wondered how the man's family would be notified. No one knew. The embassy maybe, suggested Max. The embassy maybe, replied the police. The sumo tournament was on the radio. Max had to repeat several of his answers.

It wasn't until the officers in charge brought Max's statement to their supervisor for his approval that the problems began. The supervisor, who Max never did see incidentally, would not approve the statement until he inspected Max's

101

passport or Alien Registration booklet. Max had neither. The booklet was resting snugly inside his inner left breast pocket of his suit jacket hanging in the closet of his office.

Good citizenship, repeated several officials brought in for the inquiry, implies adherence to the laws of the land. Max, they pointed out, had agreed to this when he received his visa. "It is best," they added, "for orderly society."

Max was allowed to leave the police station a few minutes after 7:00 P.M. His joint venture partner, the respected Mr. Shimizu, had brought the necessary document and had pleaded Max's case admirably. Only two apology letters were required.

"You should not forget to carry papers," scolded Mr. Shimizu as he and Max parted on the steps of the police station. "Remember, you guest here," he added.

Max went home to Homat Cornucopia, put his one LP of Australian songs on the turntable, refused dinner, and got drunk.

Let's Healthy

"Snoring Can Be Fatal, British Scientist Warns"—headline of a page three story in the Saturday, December 14 edition of the *Japan Times*. "Blood pressure soars and the heart starts to beat irregularly. Air being sucked in through the mouth causes the oropharynx to sag inward, gagging the snorer. The subsequent massive inrush of air into the lungs produces the loud gasping choke that can be heard as the heroic snore. The countless episodes when the brain's supply of oxygen is reduced eventually takes it toll."

Holy Christ.

"Study: Beer Drinkers Appear Healthier"—headline of a page six story in the Friday, December 20 edition of the *Pacific Stars and Stripes*. "The good health of beer drinkers was associated more with the regularity of drinking than with the amount consumed. Only the beer drinkers deviated significantly from the amount of illness expected in the control group. The more often people drank beer, the greater the apparent health benefit. Those who drank 15 to 34 pints (per week) had 23.5% less illness."

That's more like it.

However, the article about snoring concludes with the statement "—drink tends to promote snoring, and snorers should not drink in the evening, but only earlier in the day." The era of bacon, eggs, cornflakes and beer has arrived for the health-conscious.

Max Danger, an otherwise nice guy, was a snorer of heroic tonality. His nocturnal eruptions—the old sagging oropharynx—duplicated all the sounds of nature in the jungle. This fact was confirmed not only by the beautiful Gloria, whose dreams often featured helicopters and heavy earth-moving machinery, but by complete strangers in the neighborhood of Max's slumbers. The entire wing of patients in the Red Cross hospital, for example, knew when Max dropped off at night and awoke in the morning. Fellow passengers in flight would request transfers to other sections of the aircraft whenever he dozed.

Max Danger, still a nice guy, was also a beer drinker of heroic proportions. When one considers the alternatives in Japan—Campari soda tasting like candy, water-diluted whisky tasting like detergent, *shochu* tasting like anything

103

from peppermint sticks to chocolate cupcakes—beer is not a bad compromise. At least it always tastes the same, and for the marathon sessions after work, its effects can be quantified.

The irony of all this is that one memorable evening—during a "production seminar" with key staff in a hot springs area near Hakone—snoring saved Max's life and beer nearly killed him.

Once a year, Max's company sales staff went to an *onsen* area to blow off steam. Salesmen in Japan deserve this kind of thing. To get individuals willing to leave the comfort of the group and the office, and to walk out as individuals to flog a product, is by no means easy. Particularly if they're university graduates.

Max was flattered to have been invited on the trip by his band of corporate samurai. It would mean a two-hour trip in a smoke-filled train on a Friday after work. It would mean a 9:00 P.M. dinner on the floor after arrival at the hot springs (and after the first session in the scalding baths). It would mean giving an inspirational speech, listening to other inspirational speeches, and then individually toasting all forty of the participants. It would mean maintaining the appearance of being highly amused by the antics of aged geisha whose little tricks and mild obscenities must have been titillating before the era of pornographic comics and live sex on Channel 12.

Most importantly, Max's invitation demonstrated that he was beginning to be accepted by the group. He would be leaving the realm of rigid hierarchical levels in the office, and entering the opposite world of absolute and complete equality of Japanese men on a bender. And he would be sharing a tatami room at night with eight of his fellow equals.

The trip went as expected. The fun and games with the geisha, the marathon bouts of mah jong, and the snack food/whisky and water consumption began to wind down about 2:00 in the morning. Some of the sensible souls were already curled up on futons—the less sensible ones stepping over, upon and around them in quest of the last snack or final drop of Suntory. The floor was ankle-deep in trash.

Max, and a couple of die-hards, made a last trip to the bath. The outdoor section was the best place—viewing stars through the rising steam was relaxing and peaceful. Had he not been drowsy, Max could have stayed there all night.

Returning to his room, Max groped around in the dark searching for an empty futon. He found one against the wall near the entrance to the toilet. Democracy.

He was just dropping off—or perhaps he had been asleep for a minute or two—when he felt a hard object bounce off his shoulder. Seasoned snorers are accustomed to things being thrown at them, and Max barely gave it a thought. The futon was comfortable, and Max quickly descended into the arms of Morpheus. He was oblivious to everything, until the firemen arrived.

Awakening suddenly from a deep sleep is often disorienting—even if it happens in your own bed. Awakening suddenly in a roomful of shouting, stomping strangers, red lights flashing against the wall and fire extinguishers spraying foam in random directions, can be remarkably unsettling. Max's first thought was that the world was coming to an end. Someone grabbed his arm and led him, clad merely in undershorts, down some stairs, along a corridor, and out into the dark and crisply cold early morning air. Dozens of similarly clad figures were already in the street staring at the smoke pouring from the inn. The joint was on fire.

The chaos in and around the building died down in about

an hour. The fire was confined to the kitchen area on the floor below Max's room. The smoke made matters appear to be worse than they really were.

What saved the day was the prompt notification of the fire department. What led to the prompt notification of the fire department was the early detection of smoke in the sleeping area. What led to the early detection of smoke in the sleeping area was the wide-awake condition of three of Max's colleagues—two from his room and one from the next room—who were meeting in the hall to discuss the problem of the *gaijin's* snoring and the fact that it could be heard all over that section of the inn. As it turned out, *not* snoring could have been fatal.

Oh boy, were there ever a lot of laughs over that turn of events. Shivering in the lobby, as much from nerves as from the cold, the guests of the inn stood around chattering and laughing for a while after the firemen left. Several of the guests slapped Max on the back in mock appreciation for his role in the episode. The *ibiki* (it means "snore," folks) champion! Ho, ho.

Someone called for a beer. It was 5:30 in the morning. The wife of the inn's owner, a tiny little lady, went over to a pile of plastic beer bottle cases twice her height and began to wrestle out bottles. Max, the tallest man in the building, gallantly nudged the little lady aside. He reached for a bottle. The cases, no doubt disturbed in their balance by the recent commotion in the lobby, tipped. On Max. Dozens of the big bottles. Crashing and exploding. It was nearly the end of Max Danger, Expat.

The Expense Account

"BUSINESS ENTERTAINMENT," the classic expense account phrase, refers to a range of activities too broad for the covers of any book.

There are generalities that can be applied in describing the subject, standard maneuvers and patterns which can be enumerated and catalogued, but a comprehensive examination of the phenomenon would be a compilation of the Human Experience.

Somewhere along the line, a primitive ancestor discovered that it was not always necessary to bash over the head with a boulder the short-man-with-long-arms-and-wrinkled-fingers-who-lives-by-the-place-where-the-water-flows in order to eat the man's fish. He could be persuaded to part with his extra fish in return for the fur of the jump-prancer-who-runs-in-the-woods-and-doesn't-mind-the-snow.

Things probably went well at first until either the balance of supply and demand tipped, or the market place was disturbed by the arrival of the new guy with wash and wear loincloths. Competition entered the picture, and business entertainment was born. ("May I get you another glass of clear-fluid-with-berserk-making-properties on the rocks with an olive, Mr. Fish Man?") The expense account was created shortly thereafter as a dodge to fool the despicable-one-who-crawls-out-from-beneath-rocks-and-works-for-the-Internal Revenue Service.

To understand the ramifications of business entertainment, and thus the subtleties of expense account preparation, one must be hip to the business and cultural climate in which the activities occur. Imagine Nero's difficulties—had the Roman Empire been part of a Chicago-based conglomerate—in explaining the details of, and the necessity for, an orgy. ("But slave girls and grapes are crucial for proper atmosphere.") How many pyramids would have been built had the Pharoahs been required to obtain approval from an accounts clerk in London? ("They're going to be big pointy things, and the construction work will solve our unemployment problem for decades.")

Max Danger, Expat, found the situation in Japan—vis-à-vis his head office—to be not unlike that described above. The problem was exacerbated by the mind-set of an accounting department vice-president, who had never been west of Pennsylvania or east of Brooklyn. He earned less per month than Max's Tokyo rent, he had never spent more than 60 cents for a cup of coffee, his kids went to the neighbourhood school, but he was a corporate vice-president and sat in a corner office.

The accountant thought Max's first two expense reimbursement submissions were crude jokes and he sent them back with "Ha Ha" written in big letters across the pages. The first Cost of Living Allowance check Max received from the man was a month late and included the statement in the accompanying memo, "I have been told to send this but I am on record as not being responsible when the error is discovered."

In order to deal with these watchdogs of corporate coffers, Max created a glossary condensing a range of normal Japan business practices into the type of phraseology head office accountants more or less accept. (It's not easy out here in the field.)

NORMAL PRACTICE: Trip to Shinjuku to dissuade a distributor from increasing fees. Man's face, therefore, lost. Dinner at restaurant of his choice to demonstrate "concern" (and, in effect, to apologize for catching him price-gouging). Giggling girls, saké, sit on the floor. Post-dinner disco, pre-mixed whisky and water, more giggling girls. Distributor's toupee trampled underfoot during spirited Beach Boys number. Gigglers reach hysterics, thereby increasing thirst. Post-dinner, post-disco club to examine toupee. Napoleon brandy. Johnny Walker Black for the piano player. Gigglers receive taxi fare home—to the very extremes of Honshu. Distributor agrees to roll back fees but concerned about cost of toupee. Two more rounds of drinks "for the road." Face regained.

EXPENSE-ACCOUNT ENTRY:
Cocktails and dinner, ¥189, 450
Transportation, ¥81,800
New rug for office, ¥49,999

NORMAL PRACTICE: Major "friend of corporation" on trip to Japan from Europe. Has blessings of head office hot shots. Wants to know which girls in office "single." Saw *Hiroshima, Mon Amour* in original uncut version. Related to Don Juan. Asks if Hotel Okura objects to guests in room. Away from family 48 hours. Trip to "soapland." Back in hotel asleep by 9:15 P.M.

EXPENSE-ACCOUNT ENTRY:
Health Club Membership Fees, ¥40,000

NORMAL PRACTICE: Ministry official agrees to dinner. Dinner, however, cannot be in Tokyo. Osaka is suggested. Sensitivity of meeting is noted, importance of license is appreciated. Bullet train tickets in plain brown envelope. Saturday night family plans cancelled. Traditional inn is booked. Geisha and *samisen* encouraged. License not discussed, but eventually approved.

Expense-Account Entry:

License Application Fee, ¥300,000

Normal Practice: Middle-level Japanese employees depressed. Sense of the group is that *gaijin* management too remote. A drink after work to right real and/or imagined wrongs. Pizza, chicken on a stick, fresh soy beans ("Danger-san, you shouldn't eat whole thing—just bean inside"), fried eels, breaded crab legs, sliced salmon *sandos,* and raw carrot sticks ordered and semi-consumed before first drinks arrive. (Waiter with tray of six beers, six Campari sodas, and a Beefeater Martini on the rocks with a twist asks who gets the Beefeater Martini on the rocks with a twist.) Later to karaoke bar, more beer, sticks of chocolate, and over a dozen renditions of "I Did It My Way." Finally to hostess bar, VSOP whisky, more beer, Mama-san loves *gaijin* and had one as boyfriend after war, sudden saké, several drop-outs due to illness—one of them spectacularly erupting at the table, close the place at 1:00 A.M. Everyone friends.

Expense-Account Entry:

Employee Welfare Fund Contribution, ¥169,410

Normal Practice:

Visit from immediate head office supervisor. All of the foregoing.

Expense Account Entry:

None.

Differences

"WE ARE DIFFERENT," say the Japanese. If Max had heard that once, he had heard it—in varying contexts—every single day since the move to Tokyo.

"Being different" is, depending on the circumstances and locale, wonderful. It explains away a multitude of misunderstandings and errors in communication. It reinforces vaguely held beliefs. It becomes the ultimate answer in any attempt to unravel by debate the root causes of most types of behavior.

It is, for the Japanese, an aspect of national consciousness. Awareness of the "difference" underlies all encounters with things, and people, foreign. The degree of "difference" becomes the rule by which alien ideas and conduct are measured. It can be very, very comfortable.

It goes without saying, of course, that the satisfaction of "being different" is dependent upon circumstances and locale. A fully-dressed insurance salesman in a nudist colony would be as uncomfortable as a naked man in a red beanie and black slippers at a College of Cardinals session in the Vatican. One must have numbers on one's side.

Within Japan, the numbers are there. (If the population of Japan were to be related to time, the number of *gaijin* in a 24-hour period would be the equivalent of one minute and nine seconds.) Nothing wrong with "being different" under those circumstances—particularly if the other 23

111

hours 58 minutes and 51 seconds share essentially identical beliefs.

Something more than just "being different," Max discovered, was involved in the way of things in Japan. Each nation on this planet has customs and practices that are unique to the territory. The cannibalism of Borneo until recent years was a special treat not fully appreciated in Boston tearooms. The political intrigue in all the New World countries below Mexico does not make sense to the average Swede in the street. (There have been, in fact, more el Presidentos, dictators, premiers, and military governors south of the border than there *are* Swedes in the street.)

Middle Easterners bargain in bazaars; German shopkeepers set the price, and the price is the price. Greeks break crockery at banquets. Brits drink port and go to bed with each others' wives. Australians pour beer on their heads and toss (meaning throw) dwarfs for laughs. The French are French. It is all a richly varied, and not easily interchangeable tapestry of human behavior.

However, and this is a big however, folks, barring the influences of organized religion—which the Japanese don't have anyway—all the "differences" that make other peoples unique, are differences that generally fall in the "what the hell, that's the way things are done around here" category. Not throwing crockery at a banquet just seems to make sense to an Englishman. To a Greek, throwing things seems to be fun. Nothing particularly mystical is involved.

But the Japanese, in Max's opinion, see their "difference" differently. They *believe* it. Now whether or not they *are* different is not the point. Certainly, a large tribe of humanity completely isolated on an island and browbeaten by despots for a long time is bound to grow up strange. It is difficult to get in step with the rest of the world without having experienced the upheaval of industrial revolution, the thrill

112

of invasion, the agony of assimilation, the puzzle of political self-determination, or the comforts of corporate organized religion.

Yet really believing in a "difference"—a special uniqueness—results in a pattern of behavior that must be recognized and coped with if outsiders are to be successful in local endeavors. Max's approach is to accept the pattern of behavior for what it is, and avoid the debate on the bogus issue of "difference." In business, it works slightly more than half the time. That puts one ahead of the game.

"You don't understand, Danger-san. We are different from you people."

The remark, from the leader of Max's company union, was made in response to management's offer of a 5.5 percent salary increase.

"We Japanese do not just want money like Western workers."

"What then?" asked Max, anticipating the answer that had been given each day for the better part of the three-week negotiation.

"We Japanese speak in a loud voice to share with the company any of the profits of our workers' doings."

"Management agrees," said Max. "And you know our profits. We therefore offer 5.5 percent increase."

Max listened quietly during the 15 minute lecture on how the special effects of rice-culture sharing of labor and dividends developed an innate sense of fairness implicit in all Japanese employer-employee relationships, and how Westerners had to try to appreciate these special circumstances.

"But 5.5 percent is fair," Max suggested at the conclusion of the lecture.

Max listened quietly during the ten minute report on how

113

Western hunter-gatherers developed individualistic instincts incompatible with societal organization, making it difficult for them to appreciate the subtleties of complete "human" cooperation.

"You don't realize, but we Japanese must feel that your offer is genuine."

"Fair enough," thought Max, as he left the bargaining session. He and the union leader took the elevator together down to the lobby. The management and the union support committees remained behind in the conference room, absorbed in *obento* dinners. The negotiations had gone on for about as long as was reasonably possible to expect.

"How much do you need?" asked Max, knowing Watanabe-san had to cover himself.

"5.9 percent and a ¥10,000 increase in the Section Chief allowance," was the reply.

"You can have the allowance, but 5.7 percent is the maximum salary increase," said Max.

"Okay," confirmed Watanabe-san as the doors opened to the darkened lobby.

The negotiations were concluded the following day. The only real "difference" Max could spot was that after the final session, both sides went out together to drink beer and eat chicken on a stick.

An International Affair

"WHAT'S A VIRGIN, Daddy?"

"Urp," responded the quick-thinking Max Danger, Expat. The family was at the dinner table.

114

"Do you know, Daddy?"

"Er, well, yes, I do know. Ah, why do you ask?"

"I just want to be one," replied eight-year-old Mona, the middle Danger offspring.

"Eat your carrots, darling," suggested the beautiful Gloria with motherly concern.

"Don't worry, Mona, you are one," confided the eldest child, a young man of twelve whose worldliness grew with each day's trip to and from the American School.

"Can I be one too?" asked the youngest Danger, whose wordliness receded with each day's session in the neighborhood kindergarten.

"Eat your carrots, all of you," reminded the beautiful Gloria.

The family applied itself to the carrots.

"Are you sure I am one, Daddy?"

"Yes, I am sure, sweetheart. My, aren't these carrots good."

Potatoes were passed, bread was consumed, milk was spilled—all in relative silence. The family members were each lost in private thoughts.

"Are we a good family?" asked Mona, after a moment or two.

"Of course we are," answered Gloria.

"Why do you ask?" queried Max, attempting to find the thread.

"I just want to be sure," replied Mona, the pile of carrots growing on her plate in proportion to the other items of food.

Milk was spilled again.

"Eat your carrots, Mona," commanded the beautiful Gloria, "or else you won't grow up to be big and strong."

"I don't want to grow up to be big and strong," Mona blurted out, jumping from her chair and running to the

115

bedroom. "I'm already getting too big," she added before slamming the door.

Clearly a crisis was developing. Mona had always been, in Max's opinion, the most level-headed of the children. The outburst was as unlikely coming from her as anything sensible coming from the youngest, who was now stuffing carrots into his ears.

Alas, people change. Growing up is an arduous ordeal through which most adults have traveled. Increased awareness of the Big World Out There brings its joys and sorrows, its expectations and frustrations.

In response to a third grade assignment in school, Mona had diligently pored through the *Japan Times* for an item of interest for a classroom report. The papers from around the first of the year provided the most enticing item of interest. The little stories on the subject were accompanied by pictures. The more she thought about it, the more Mona became intrigued by the whole thing. She made her report in school, but kept track of the subject afterwards.

Children have the marvelous ability to envision things limited only by the boundaries of their imagination. Adults usually lose this ability, which is probably just as well if fields are to be plowed, bacon brought home, and garbage taken out. Flights of fancy contribute little to the Gross National Product.

But at eight years of age, Mona Danger's imagination was boundless. She was "in love." The lucky object of her ardor was none other than the current grandson of, and the man destined to become, the Emperor of Japan. The dashing Prince Hiro had stolen her heart.

Now you may chuckle, folks, at the absurdity of it all, but are not the stories of childhood replete with tales of handsome princes and fair damsels in remarkably romantic encounters? Fortuitously kissed frogs, Beauties asleep,

116

glass slippers at midnight—are these not the stuff of dreams? In fact, did not the selfsame Prince Hiro's parents meet at forty-love on the Karuizawa courts of tennis?

Well then, Mona's infatuation with a young gentleman residing a few kilometers from Homat Cornucopia—a gentleman for whom big things were in store—was anything but absurd.

"His car doesn't have to stop at stoplights," reported Mona during an "airing out" session with Max later the same evening. "And he gets good seats at sumo," she added. "He'll be like a king someday."

"I know, Mona, but he must find a Japanese wife," said Max.

"No, he doesn't. He can speak English. He went to school in England."

"Yes, but he must find a Japanese wife who will be the first lady of Japan—and also be shorter than he is."

"Why?"

"Because that's what people want him to do," explained Max.

They were sitting on the bed in Mona's room. A newspaper photograph of the Prince, proper and erect, was tacked to the wall. Disney characters and Michael Jackson surrounded him.

"He can do whatever he wants if he's a prince," reasoned Mona.

"But he must have a Japanese wife," said Max. They looked at the photograph in silence.

"You said I was a virgin, and I *am* shorter than he is," said Mona finally. "That's what he has to find."

"How tall are you, Mona?" Max asked.

"And you said we are a good family," continued Mona, ignoring the question.

"Well, we are a good family, but the Prince must marry

117

someone from a family with a famous name in Japan."

"It's not my fault that 'Danger' isn't famous in Japan. It is at my school."

"That's good," agreed Max, "but the real problem is that you are too young. The Prince must get married in the next year or two."

"Why?"

"Because the newspapers say so," said Max, after a pause.

"And the people?"

"And the people."

Mona stood up and smoothed the corners of the newspaper clipping.

"You know, Mona, being an emperor is an important job. He must be the symbol of the country and represent the spirit of the people. The Prince must devote his life to learning how to do the job properly."

"I know that, Daddy."

"You might not be happy," continued Max, "living like he will have to live. Like a bird in a cage."

"But if he's the Prince, can't he make the cage any size he wants?" asked Mona. Max stared at his level-headed eight-year-old daughter.

"No, he can't, sweetheart."

"Because of the people?"

"Because of the people."

Mona sat down on the bed again.

"I hate carrots, don't you, Daddy?"

"With a passion," confirmed Max.

"It's kinda sad, isn't it," said Mona, looking at the newspaper clipping.

"Yes, it is," said Max.

"Oh well," Mona sighed, bouncing to her feet and heading for the door, "I guess I don't have to worry about being a virgin."

The Package

EXPATS ARE NOT all alike.

Yes, of course, some are taller than others, some fatter, some smarter, some happier. Some are raising young families, some are on the final corporate fling before retirement. Some have a healthy attitude about life in the big T., some are being gradually eaten away by rage and frustration. Some read the *Weekender,* some (unaccountably) do not. Some expats don't even work for IBM.

But the distinction between expats is more fundamental. It is not as obvious, in Max Danger's opinion, as height, weight, family commitments, adaptability, and/or literary tastes. (Some of Max's best friends read Harold Robbins.)

It is a basic distinction that separates people in their reactions to ordinary events at cocktail parties, in the aisles of National Azabu Supermarket, at PTA meetings, and during the countless American Club functions. It creates grief for some, anxiety for others, and is of no consequence to the fortunate few.

It dictates social commitments, family plans, and business performance. It bears no relationship to intelligence, talent, or individual skills.

The distinction between expats is in the terms of the "package"—the overseas employment deal. It is a rarely discussed subject, but its effects are amazingly pervasive.

Max finds that it is convenient to categorize the expat

119

"packages"—if for no other reason than to anticipate reactions in an otherwise surface homogeneity. Naturally there are exceptions, but not many.

PACKAGE 1: Employer has "limited experience abroad" and therefore believes, out of ignorance, the description of the financial horrors visited upon the plucky expat in far off Tokyo. Normal little extras—a Mercedes Benz and driver, maids, a gardener, stock options, semi-annual home leave trips, deferred income banked in Switzerland, and a business entertainment clothing allowance for the wife—are made available to the expat warrior as he plants the corporate flag at the very edge of the earth. Fortunately for the rest of the expat community, this phenomenon is slowly fading. However, vestigial pockets of activity can still be observed at Maxim's and in the first-class sections of Tokyo-New York flights.

PACKAGE 2: Employer is a major corporation with an extensive overseas branch network and an international personnel department attuned to monitoring cost-of-living fluctuations. The terms of the package are described in a manual somewhere, and they take into account a) the specific assignment abroad and b) the employee's rank within the corporation. Naturally, the terms are diabolically designed to be "not quite enough," but at least they're depressingly clear.

PACKAGE 3: Employer is a "limited experience abroad" organization like the one offering Package 1. However, expectations as to performance and expenses differ. In the Package 3 category, it is not understood how the new office in Tokyo should be any different from the new office in

Omaha. The rent, school tuition, and American Club fees equal the total preliminary anticipation of all business expenses (including employee salaries) for an entire year.

PACKAGE 4: Employer is self. Expat survival in Japan is solely dependent upon agile wit, raw nerve, guile, flexibility in crisis, and blithe ignorance of the consequences of failure. Into this category also fall international school teachers and Regular Members of the Foreign Correspondents' Club who, unburdened by the requirement to "keep up appearances," must nevertheless keep body and soul together on less than most expense accounts in Packages 1, 2, and 3.

With the foregoing in mind, now appreciate the fiscal and social considerations behind the seemingly simple statement: "Let's get the whole group together and have cocktails and hors d'oeuvres at our house before the dance."

To sort this out, Max devised a series of tests—observations really—to clarify the expat distinctions and thereby anticipate behavior.

Shoes
PACKAGE 1   Always new
PACKAGE 2   New in Fall, old in pre-home leave Spring
PACKAGE 3   New every other year
PACKAGE 4   Hush Puppies

Travel
PACKAGE 1   Hong Kong for sightseeing
PACKAGE 2   Hong Kong for shopping
PACKAGE 3   Hong Kong on the way home
PACKAGE 4   Yokohama

*

121

Sunday Evening Dinner

PACKAGE 1   Keyaki Grill at the Capitol Tokyu Hotel
PACKAGE 2   American Club
PACKAGE 3   Moti's Indian Restaurant
PACKAGE 4   Someone's house

Golden Week Whereabouts

PACKAGE 1   Kyoto traditional inn
PACKAGE 2   Hawaii
PACKAGE 3   Guam
PACKAGE 4   Tokyo

Length of Assignment

PACKAGE 1   Until someone catches on in the head office
PACKAGE 2   3.2 years
PACKAGE 3   Day by day
PACKAGE 4   When fortune made

Headache Source

PACKAGE 1   Possible confusion over Pan Am/United direct flight to New York schedules.
PACKAGE 2   Alcohol
PACKAGE 3   No expense reimbursement checks for two months
PACKAGE 4   The specter of bankruptcy

Japanese Friendships

PACKAGE 1   Driver
PACKAGE 2   —
PACKAGE 3   All the guys in the office
PACKAGE 4   Neighborhood bartender, partner's wife, loan manager at Sanwa bank, *ramen* delivery boy.

	Reading Matter
PACKAGE 1	Wall Street Journal
PACKAGE 2	Internal company publications
PACKAGE 3	Help Wanted ads in trade magazines
PACKAGE 4	Science fiction

	Frequent Foods
PACKAGE 1	Filet Mignon
PACKAGE 2	Filet of Sole
PACKAGE 3	Cheeseburger
PACKAGE 4	Curry rice

	Attire for the Chamber of Commerce Dance
PACKAGE 1	Black Tie and Tux
PACKAGE 2	Black Tie and Tux
PACKAGE 3	Black Tie and Tux
PACKAGE 4	Black Tie and Tux (with Hush Puppies)

John Bates

IT WAS COLD the day John Bates died.

One meets a broad range of people and personalities in the panorama of expat life in Japan. The professional and business skills required for jobs abroad guarantee an expat population comfortable with adapting and achieving under conditions somewhat more complex than those at home. Overseas assignments distinguish people from those whose lifestyles involve sitting on the front porch in the gathering dusk, chewing Red Man tobacco, and spitting into the bushes.

But despite the lofty professional and business credentials, there are nevertheless all types of characters in the expat group. It's Mother Nature's way of keeping us on our toes. There are good guys, there are middle-of-the-road guys, and there are jerks. John Bates was one of the good guys.

Running a business that retails products to both Japanese and foreign consumers means pretty deep involvement in the bi-cultural subtleties and machinations of the market-place. It means motivating unicultural salesmen and skeptical distributors. It means hanging around with the staff until all hours of the night and early morning. It means showing up, seriously hung over, at 7:30 hotel breakfast meetings with visiting head office dignitaries. It means listening to all kinds of advice—good and bad. It is a fairly normal manifestation of expat responsibilities. John Bates did that sort of thing well.

He also found a considerable amount of time to devote to an active family—a wife, and four grade and high school children. John Bates showed up at the swim meets, soccer matches, little league baseball games, school plays, and recitals. He, like many, suffered through the heat and the chill, the triumphs and the disasters typical of that involvement.

He took his wife off on mini-trips now and then, waltzed under the stars, and most certainly promised to slow down soon. He supported her efforts to start a small importing business in Tokyo.

In his spare time, John Bates served on school committees and the American Club board. He organized things—primarily for the youth and teens of the community. He always went to the damn meetings.

Max Danger first met John Bates in yet another role.

They played tennis together. They argued over line calls, ridiculed each other's serves, hit to each other's backhands, and drank beer together in the club house afterwards. There they wagered on significant matters—the relative population of sheep to humans in John Bates' native New Zealand.

The man became a good guy, in Max's opinion, by doing something relatively unusual. Although a half-dozen or more years of active involvement in local things kept him busy, John Bates was still willing to spend the precious commodity of time with a newcomer who was green as grass and did not know the Keidanren from Kabuki. Max learned the techniques of survival in the big T. because John Bates, an experienced expat, sat still and answered questions.

John Bates died suddenly, in the prime of life, at age 40. "Complications," it was announced, "due to minor surgery." These things happen. He had beaten Max 6–4, 6–3 the day before. The next tennis match had been scheduled for what turned out to be the day of the funeral. It was cold that day also.

The services were held in the chapel of the International School of the Sacred Heart—up the hill from Hiroo. Walking up that hill, Max was struck by the sheer number of people whose lives had been entwined with John Bates. Hundreds of people were crowding into the chapel. There were batches of children from several different schools led by somber teachers. There were children with parents. Business associates and competitors crunched across the gravelled walk together.

There were people who served on committees with John Bates, went to church with him, lived next to him, sang and danced with him. There were probably a few enemies in the crowd, there were certainly more than a few plain old pals. It was to be expected, of course, but Max was unprepared for the emotional impact apparent in the circumstances.

Communal grief is a rare and alien experience in the ex-pat world. Because most expat families are in the prime of life, death is usually relegated to a private arena of personal anguish suffered by individuals whose families and friends back home are hit. An expat will disappear for a week or so, and return with only the bittersweet memory of a loved one lost. The community may notice, but seldom partici-pates.

Living abroad is unreal in this respect. All societies have more or less elaborate rituals for the basic occasions of birth, marriage and death. People seem to need it, and so-ciety is thereby strengthened. But what an awful thing is a funeral for one communally loved, admired and respected.

The service, lasting about an hour, seemed interminable. Max stared at his hands, the flowers, the burning candles. He glanced once or twice at the black-framed picture of John Bates—a Japanese touch—perched behind his coffin. In fact, he could not look at the face in the photograph, only the necktie. Max's eyes met no one's in the chapel, none met his.

The priest addressed words of comfort to the brand new widow, the kids, parents, and in-laws. Seemingly futile sounds tossed in the air. The school children began to cry. The priest concluded his remarks, looking out over the crowd, with the statement: "And as you all know, John Bates was a good man." Max could barely breathe.

The several hundred attendees stood in the cold outside the chapel at the conclusion of the services. Except for the sound of crunching gravel under shifting feet, there was ab-solute silence. The ritual was over, but no one left.

Fifteen minutes later, the coffin and the immediate family emerged from the chapel. The family members seemed sur-prised that anyone was around—let alone several hundred.

126

One of the Bates children began to cry—a neighbor standing nearby picked up the child and hugged her. Max looked up at the trees. The December wind in his face made his eyes water. The black cars eventually drove off—the front one carrying the remains of John Bates, a good guy.

Only the squawking damn crows made noise as the crowd dispersed. Most people, in family groups of two, three or four, shuffled down the hill to Hiroo. Looking back on it later, Max figured the scene must have resembled a Fellini movie without sound.

The hustle and bustle of a Saturday afternoon crowd in Hiroo—alive, colorful, animated—was momentarily shocking to the senses. Kids rode bicycles two abreast on the narrow sidewalk, scattering pedestrians. An old man, older by 40 years than John Bates, carried garbage cans out to the edge of the street. John Bates was already on the way to his land of sheep. Max suddenly realized he still owed him ¥10,000 for the sheep vs. people bet made earlier in the week.

The Danger family struggled past the crowds massed at the subway entrance—folks were studying the fare map as if they had never seen it before. John Bates really was a good guy. Max noticed, in the crowd, a man he recognized from the funeral. His back was to Max, and he was leaning against the wall next to the ticket machines. His shoulders were hunched over and he was coughing, or something.

Max made it all the way to the corner—the corner where the cookie store is now—before he broke down.

The Holiday Visitors, Part I

THE BEAUTIFUL Gloria Danger's parents, Cedric and Violet
Malone, announced their plans for the big holiday trip to
Japan. Gloria was ecstatic. The kids were excited. Max knew
it would happen sooner or later.

Cedric Malone, upon whom retirement was a new and ill-
fitting cloak, was a big man in Pittsburgh. Of humble
beginnings, Cedric had parlayed a numbers operation in
the steel mills into a chain of liquor stores and pawn shops
that earned for him not only the respect of friends and
neighbors, but enough loot to buy 24-hour protection from
his customers and enemies. Gloria was his only daughter,
Max was his only son-in-law. Gloria was the apple of his
eye. Max was a rapist, and because of the move to Japan,
a kidnapper as well.

Violet Malone had blue hair and was nice. Between 1946
and 1985 she had given, by her own reckoning, piano lessons
to 451 of the 657 children born and raised within a three-mile
radius of her front parlor. A musical rakehell, she had learned in her flaming youth to play Schubert's Impromptu Opus
142, D. 935, in A flat. *Backwards.*

From the early days of his marriage, Max had problems
settling on names for his in-laws. "Mom" and "Dad" were
out of the question. First names were equally inappropriate
because Max and Gloria had begun dating in high school.
The disparity between Max's and his in-laws' stations in

life at that time had locked Max into a pattern of formality difficult to break. The arrival of children eased the situation somewhat—Max began referring to Gloria's parents with the names used by the children for their grandparents. The children, unfortunately, were slowly abandoning those names. In fact, Max was now the only one regularly calling Cedric "Poopaw" and Violet "Mumpsie."

"Let's take them to Disneyland," exclaimed the youngest Danger, an opportunist.

"Let's take them to Omote Sando," offered the middle child, a female and born shopper.

"Let's take them camping in Hokkaido," suggested the oldest offspring, a youngster in whom Max was beginning to recognize uncomfortably familiar off-the-wallisms.

"Let's plan a cocktail party," added Gloria, "and invite all our new friends."

"Good ideas, all of you," replied Max. "But before we plan anything, let's make sure they get a decent room at the Hotel Okura."

"The Okura? My parents are not staying at the Okura. My parents are staying here," announced Gloria.

"Not in my room," from the opportunist.

"Not in my room," from the shopper.

"How about a tent in the living room?" from the oldest.

"Not in our room," from Max, although that is where the Malones eventually landed. (Max was later to report that the futon in the utility room was surprisingly comfortable, but that the cat's litter box should have been moved some-place else—Denver, for example.)

Plans for the big visit proceeded. Halls were decked with ivy boughs. A Christmas tree, cut in August by farmers in Aomori who must find it amusing that foreigners put those things inside their houses, was ordered and paid for. The cost approximated Max's weekly salary at the time their oldest was born. Special attention was paid to gifts and presents—Bing Crosby records were dug out of storage and dusted off. It really would be a merry old Christmas. Families should be together at this time of the year. At least for a while.

"There they are. There they are," proclaimed the youngest.

The Danger family was at Narita.

"I saw them first," said the middle child.

"No, you didn't."

"Yes, I did."

"No, you didn't."

"Yes, I did."

"Shut up," Max explained.

The Dangers, along with several thousand other visitors, were waiting outside the customs area, catching only brief glimpses of the baggage inspection counters through the swinging doors. It had been a long wait. Many flights, delayed earlier in the day, were now arriving with flights normally scheduled for this time. The Malones had been on a plane which had arrived more or less on time, but that was over two hours ago. Max could imagine the chaos behind the doors. The Japanese, with a tendency to scurry in the best of times, can create human and baggage gridlock when things are running late. Max could also imagine his father-in-law—a man with the patience of a hand grenade—turning crimson with frustration. "He's liable to punch somebody," Max thought to himself. "I hope the kids don't see it."

"Grandpa, Grandma," shouted the children as the Malones finally made it through the doors.

"Hi Dad, Mom," said Gloria, hugging them both.

"Hello Poop—er, sir," said Max, shaking Cedric's hand.

"Let me help you with that bag, Mrs., ah, Mumpsie."

Things went well for seven or eight minutes.

"Whataya mean we gotta take a two hour bus ride to Tokyo," queried Cedric. "Did we get off at the wrong airport?"

The situation regarding Narita's position on this planet was explained.

"Whataya mean we gotta take a half hour taxi ride to your house."

The situation regarding the Tokyo City Air Terminal's position in Japan was explained.

"Where's the other half of your apartment?" was the question after unloading at Homat Cornucopia. Max did not explain the apartment situation in Tokyo. After all the years of being involved with the beautiful Gloria's family, Max knew that her father was three-fourths bluster. (Her mother, meanwhile, would be happy in a broom closet provided, of course, it contained a piano.)

The "settling in" process went smoothly—frankly the Malones were exhausted after the trip, their first venture outside the continental U.S. of A. The kids had gone to bed. Gloria and her mother were in the master bedroom involved in "girl talk." Max and his father-in-law sat in the living room by the fire.

"We're planning a trip to the Nissan auto assembly plant," explained Max.

"Good," said Cedric.

"We'll do some shopping in the Ginza," offered Max. "The Christmas decorations are remarkably well done."

"Good," said Cedric.

"I'd like you to come to the office and meet the staff," suggested Max.

"Good," said Cedric.

They both stared at the fire—the popping and snapping

of the burning logs being the only sound in the room. All the lights were off.

"Can I get you more bourbon?" asked Max.

"Yes," said Cedric, not taking his eyes from the fire.

More popping and snapping.

"Look, my boy," said Cedric. "There is one thing I'd like to do."

"Name it," replied Max.

"It's as much for the guys back home as it is for me."

"I can imagine," said Max, not imagining. The one-fourth of Cedric which was not bluster was emerging.

"I'd like to—you know," said Cedric to his son-in-law, the rapist.

"You'd like to what?" asked Max.

Pop. Snap.

"I'd like to, you know, while I'm here, you know—make it with a geisha."

The Holiday Visitors, Part II

AMONG THE GREAT things about living abroad is the heady feeling of satisfaction one gets whenever the little mysteries and puzzles of local life are solved. Adaptation to environment is a primal instinct, and man's particular successes in this regard have resulted in the dominance of *homo sapiens* over tree sloths and lizards in top hats.

Japan does more than most countries to provide Westerners with opportunities for this heady feeling of satisfaction. Think how mundane things would be if one could really read the signs—even the ones in English. Think how simple it would all become—boring probably—if one understood what the policeman with the orange stick was ranting and raving about. What if "yes" really meant yes? We just might be replaced by lizards in top hats.

There is another dimension to this. Any foreigner with six months' experience in Japan has an enormous advantage over first-time visitors. The mysteries thrown up by the Japanese are at first awesome. To be a Tokyo veteran, for whatever time, gives one power. And power changes relationships.

To test this, take a first-time visitor—whether it be the chairman of your company, your former parole officer, or a rich uncle—to the Shibuya shopping area on a Saturday afternoon. Start walking in any direction from the statue of the obsessive-compulsive dog. Suddenly disappear. Watch the panic develop within seconds on the face of your visitor as he is swept along on the black-haired tide of scurrying humanity. The look of relief when you reappear will be not unlike that of a suckling infant groping for its mother's breast. You and that visitor will forever have a different relationship.

Hosting his in-laws, Cedric and Violet Malone, on their first trip to Japan, Max had countless opportunities to exhibit his mastery of the complexities of life in Tokyo. His father-in-law was beginning, for the first time ever, to look at Max with some semblance of respect, albeit respect born of total dependency.

"We'll just get on the train at this platform," said Max to Cedric, "and we'll be home in no time."

"How the hell do you know which one?" asked Cedric.

"It's easy," replied Max, "the destination is written in Japanese." Max did not mention to his father-in-law that they were waiting for the green Yamanote circle line, and

133

that getting lost on that line was impossible. He also did not point out that they had accidentally taken the long way around from Ebisu to Shinjuku, hoping that Cedric wouldn't notice the difference in traveling time if they got on the train going in the correct, and shorter, direction back home.

"You were pretty strong negotiating with the clerk in that camera store," Cedric said to Max.

"One has to be firm," replied Max. His "negotiations" had been merely a matter of repeating in Japanese the numbers quoted by the clerk from the price list. To the un-initiated, repeating ¥47,525 several times, with corrections from the clerk, might appear to be a slightly weightier discussion.

"I'm happy with the camera," said Cedric, "but I still don't know how much it costs in real money."

"We got a good deal," concluded Max, leading Cedric into the green train heading, incidentally, the long way around to Ebisu.

There is, however, something lost when one becomes a veteran of any place. One loses the ability to register distinct impressions that are new and remarkable. Max, for example, barely remembered his first encounter with the little ladies cleaning the public toilets. His father-in-law, however, was distinctly impressed—charging out of a restaurant facility horror-struck. He thereafter refused to use any rest room until Max had gone first and given the "all clear" signal.

But more than anything else, Max's in-laws were over-whelmed in their first impressions by the "cuteness" of all they observed in Japan. Gloria's mother, Violet Malone, was by nature impressed with cuteness. Fortunately for her relationship with Cedric, who abhorred cuteness, there were relatively few opportunities to observe such things in and around Pittsburgh, Pennsylvania.

"Oh look, Cedric," said Violet one evening watching

Japanese television, "aren't those bunny rabbits cute in the vodka commercial."

"Cute?" roared Cedric. "Aren't there any adults in this nation? I still haven't heard a grown woman's voice since I got here."

The trip to the Nissan automobile assembly plant—where a big deal was made of the fact that Cedric, his wife Violet, and his daughter Gloria were named after automobiles—caused Cedric to wax eloquent on the subject of cuteness.

"How can any country be successfully challenging Detroit's automakers," he reasoned, "with runty little laborers wearing women's slippers and office girls in cute knee socks and Mickey Mouse sweatshirts?"

"Cute is nice, dear," said Violet.

"If you're a twelve-year-old girl," mumbled Cedric, watching a car with dangling huggables pass them on the expressway.

As the holiday visit approached its conclusion, amidst heady feelings of satisfaction and new discoveries of cuteness, one chore remained for Max. His father-in-law wanted, as much for the guys back home as for himself, to "make it" with a geisha.

"Geishas don't do that kind of thing," said Max to Cedric one quiet afternoon. "Or at least not on a one-shot basis."

"Yes, they do," corrected Cedric. "Any of the guys in the mill who were here after the war will tell you."

"Things have changed since then," said Max.

"Ha. Buildings change, people don't."

"Why don't you just *tell* the guys back home that you 'made it' with a geisha," offered Max.

"Young man," pronounced Cedric Malone, father of the beautiful Gloria, "I don't bullshit my friends."

On that note of moral rectitude, Max and his father-in-law set off the following day—the day before the Malones'

135

departure—to the wilds of Kawasaki City. Arrangements had been made through the sensitive understanding of Max's business colleague, Serious Hirose. Two young ladies, costumed for the occasion in gowns resembling real kimono, awaited the intrepid adventurers from the West. The establishment, "Mama Peachboy," had recently undergone an adjectival name change and was now called a "soapland." Providing "total body massage" was, nevertheless, its forte.

"You just go wherever your girl takes you," said Max to his father-in-law, not really on firm ground himself. "And do whatever she does," he added. Max wondered what he'd do if the old man had a heart attack. Run, probably.

"Relax," said Cedric to Max. "I know all about this from the guys back home."

They each followed a girl off to the nether regions of the establishment.

The trip on the train back to Homat Cornucopia was spent in silence. Cedric dozed, Max stared into the middle distance. Never, thought Max, could he have imagined involving himself and his father-in-law in activities such as had occurred in the last hour. He had first met the man 20 years ago, as a teenager, parked outside the man's house with the beautiful Gloria. Cedric, Mr. Malone then, had chased Max down the street with what appeared to be at the time a meat ax. Max even had to steal back at 3:00 A.M. to retrieve his '58 Chevy. It was the night he and Gloria kissed for the first time. And here they were, roués together, in Japan. Incredible.

Dinner that evening was uneventful; the grandparents spent a lot of time with the grandchildren. Violet played the piano, Cedric regaled everyone with stories about walking to school as a child through eight-foot snow drifts. Plans

136

were made for the trek to Narita Airport the following day.

The kids finally went to bed. Gloria and her mother retired to the bedroom for one last chance to have "girl talk."

Max and Cedric sat by the fire in the living room.

"More bourbon?" asked Max.

"Thanks," said Cedric.

The logs snapped and popped. All the lights were out.

"I'm very glad you and Mump—, er, Violet could make the trip," said Max. "It was fun for everybody."

"Yes, it was," said Cedric.

Snap. Pop.

"And kid," added Cedric, "thanks for today."

"Well, I—"

"Never mind," interrupted Cedric, "we all do dumb things now and then."

"I guess so," said Max.

Snap. Pop.

"By the way," said Cedric after a few moments, "did you notice that girls here are just like girls everywhere?"

The Negotiation

THE U.S.-JAPAN trade problem may *never* be solved!

The real difficulty has little to do with yen/dollar exchange rates, voluntary or involuntary controls, barriers real or imagined. It is not a matter of "producing" vs. "consuming" economic structures.

137

The problem is that the wrong people on opposite sides are talking to each other. Not only that, the right people on the same sides are not.

For example, a trade analysis seminar in Tokyo will invariably be comprised of individuals "sensitive" to the pressures and constraints influencing their counterparts across the conference table. The Japanese negotiators will speak English; the American negotiators will have read back-issues of the *Japan Economic Journal*. After a fashion, a policy statement in textbook form will emerge which summarizes the problems and suggests solutions. An "action plan" is created.

Fine, except the negotiators have no power to implement the plan, and no one else reads their reports. The captains of industry—who do have the power to implement plans— seldom pay attention to the murmurings of subordinates "sensitive" to issues. It's the nature of the beast.

Captains of industry, be they Japanese or American, do not get to where they are by being particularly "sensitive" to anything but their own companies' competitive performance. They are products of their own business cultures, and represent the epitome of success in their separate systems.

Fierce determination, absolute dedication, contrived duplicity, an instinct for the jugular, flashes of entrepreneurial brilliance, and well-developed survival techniques are the hallmarks of industry captaincy. And these are the guys ultimately brought together by "sensitive" souls to negotiate. One might as well contemplate Disney executives and Mafia dons meeting together to discuss Hoffa's whereabouts and plans for Goofy's 50th birthday party. The wavelengths tend to diverge.

*

138

"Call me Bart," demanded Batholemew J. Holstein, CEO of a vast and powerful conglomerate. He was Max's boss' boss' boss. He and Max were seated on tatami across the low table from Toshinari Ando, CEO of a vast and powerful rival conglomerate. Ando smiled, took the saké bottle from the kimino-clad waitress, and filled Bart's cup.

"To your health, Holstein-san," he said. "Your visit to our country is good for mutual understanding."

Ando and Holstein were in charge of economic empires producing essentially the same products. They each had spent millions trying to get into each other's domestic markets. Like duelling knights of yore, they were slowly bleeding each other to death.

"And I'll call you Toshi," continued Bart.

"If it is your wish, Holstein-san," said Ando. The dinner in the exclusive Japanese restaurant was hosted by Ando and was in reciprocation for the Western luncheon hosted the day before by Bart at the American Club. At that luncheon, Ando had made noises with his soup and had ordered Beef Ragout "medium rare." He asked the waiter what possessed him to work at the club, and left his coffee, served in lieu of unavailable green tea, untouched. On the way out the door, he asked Max if there were many club members who were *not* part of the U.S. Military.

"Mutual understanding is a good thing," stated Bart. "Therefore, I can't understand why your goddam tariff regulations exist, and yet you are free to do whatever you want in my country."

A team of kimono-clad waitresses slithered into the room with plates of raw beef and vegetables. Bart announced that he wanted none of the "white stuff" meaning, most probably, the tofu. A waitress filled his saké cup.

"I believe in shooting straight," Bart went on. "You'll

139

be in big trouble, Toshi old friend, if I talk to our Congressmen about your goddam tariffs." Bart asked the waitress for a napkin. "Your people won't even get a driver's license in the States."

"We have a saying in Japan," Ando mused, arms folded and staring at an upper corner in the room, "that bamboo grows in soil unsuitable for rice."

"You're goddam right," agreed Bart, "and that's why I'm telling you like it is."

Max busied himself with sauces and condiments. The dialogue had taken an incomprehensible turn. He ate Bart's portion of the "white stuff."

"But we also say, Holstein-san—"

"Call me Bart," Bart interrupted.

"We also say, whatever is planted must be harvested."

Jesus, thought Max.

"You're goddam right again," said Bart. The kneeling waitress serving Max leaned against him and asked if he wanted more drinks. Max was still framing his answer as Bart demanded more saké for "my friend Toshi" and a bourbon on the rocks for himself.

"So we must have patience," counselled Ando, "if the fruits of our efforts are to come with the wind."

"At least, goddam it, we agree on something," said Bart. The waitress looked at Max and smiled as she served the drinks. It occurred to Max that she must have been witness to many similar meetings of high purpose, and he wondered if the conversation was any more comprehensible to her.

"I offer another toast to the spirit of international friendship," pronounced Ando, raising his saké cup. His face glowed, not unlike an over-ripe tomato.

"Fine with me," said Bart, "but you must arrange market share for us here equal to yours in our country."

"We Japanese understand your request."

140

"That's settled then," confirmed Bart, banging his empty glass down on the table, startling the kneeling waitress. "And you, young man," he added suddenly, turning to Max, "work out the details and send me a report."

It took Max several months to summon up the nerve to commit something or other to paper. Its contents were overlooked, however, in the general chaos created by Ando's company slashing wholesale prices in the States and opening a new distribution center in Chicago. Max's company countered by ordering Max to find new maufacturing facilities in Japan. It was rumored that Bart was considering another trip to Tokyo for more negotiations, but a different crisis elsewhere in the world mercifully postponed the visit.

Max accidentally ran in to the waitress from the Japanese restaurant one Saturday afternoon in Roppongi. She was wearing jeans and eating a hamburger at McDonalds. He bought her a Coke.

"Your friends must be important VIPs," she remarked.

"Yes," Max said, "they were negotiating a complicated trade agreement."

"I thought so," the waitress concluded, lighting a Kent. "But your friends will never be friends."

The Accident

BEING INVOLVED in a simple auto accident—even one without personal injuries—is less fun in Japan than you might think.

The beautiful Gloria Danger, mother of three and PTA member at three different schools, zoomed daily about the streets and alleys of Tokyo in her bright red Honda. An experienced and skilled driver, Gloria took the responsibility of motor vehicle operation seriously. The kids were always strapped to their seats, the horn was sufficiently exercised, and snow tires were kept on the car until the Rainy Season.

The Honda, purchased used from a young lady who had advertised its sale in the *Weekender,* was for its age remarkably unscathed. (The young lady, who lived in Azabu Juban, was for her age beginning to scathe. She worked evenings in the Ginza and had graduated to a Mercedes.)

The only marks on the car developed after its purchase. A series of dented scrapes appeared on the left front fender—caused by the telephone pole that attacks drivers turning right and heading up the hill from the National Azabu Supermarket parking lot. The pole had attacked Gloria either six or seven times, depending upon whether Gloria or Max was doing the counting.

Being a "Safety Driver," as we say locally, does involve a factor in addition to skill, however. That factor is plain old good luck. Without it, one's in the wrong place at the right time, or the right place at the wrong time.

Alas, the gods of vehicular fortuity deserted the beautiful Gloria one icy morning on her way with her youngest to the dentist in Shibuya. A taxi (described later by Gloria as being "lemon-yellow" in color) exercised its social commitment to flop-armed hailers everywhere by swerving diagonally from the center to the outside of three lanes in the middle of the main Shibuya intersection. A chain of five cars, in which Gloria was link number two, slammed on the brakes.

Car number one missed the taxi—more a tribute to the cab's accelerative abilities than the first driver's skill. Gloria, meanwhile, plowed into the first driver, thereby creating the original, and culpably damaging, series of incidents. Car

142

number three skidded on the ice into Gloria—cars four and five followed in sequence. From a helicopter, the scene would probably be amusing.

Within seconds, the bus following car number five contributed to the festivities by beginning a concert of horn blowing that continued unabated for the twenty-five minutes or so it took for the wounded autos to disentangle. The taxi disappeared.

The youngest Danger, safely belted, entertained the throng of onlookers by first laughing, then crying, and finally throwing up. Gloria entertained the throng by being blonde.

Gloria asked the first driver if his wife was okay. The man, whose car was decidedly damaged in the rear—the tail lights and bumper were obliterated and the trunk lid was sticking straight into the air—gave Gloria his card and told her not to worry about anything. He jumped back into his car and he and the woman sped off, trailing a stream of fuel from his gas tank. (A subsequent phone call to the man's house, a call which his wife answered, revealed that the wife did not recall the accident. "Short memory," mused Gloria.)

The cars following Gloria in the sequence suffered progressively less damage, with the fifth and last car having only a scratched bumper—not even as bad as being attacked by the National Azabu telephone pole. That fifth driver, however, expressed concern about a possible whiplash injury. He was a Japanese man in his middle fifties, wore a turtle necksweater under a tweed sports coats with leather elbow patches, and displayed his graying hair to his shoulders—à la Berkeley 1962. He explained to Gloria that he was a writer, intellectual, and resident of Moto Azabu. His "private" medical consultant would notify Gloria if there were problems.

After a great deal of wind-sucking, *meishi* exchanges, and

deep bowing, the participants in the drama went their separate ways. Despite the fact that several thousand spectators surveyed the scene—attracted by the cacaphony of horns as much as by anything else—not one policeman showed his face. A quartet of high school students, in black military garb, pushed Gloria's battered red Honda to the curb. Gloria found a telephone, and called Max.

Insurance companies know how to handle these things, and within a half-hour the company Max used was on the scene with a tow truck. Their efficiency was such that it wasn't until Gloria and her youngest had walked to the dentist's office that she discovered her purse was still in the now-disappeared Honda. Another call to Max's office revealed that he had already departed on his overnight trip to Osaka. Max's secretary would not hazard a guess as to which insurance company he used. The problem was not the dentist, who would bill for the work performed, but the front door of the apartment in Homat Cornucopia. Gloria's keys had also been in the car.

Things that are potentially difficult elsewhere can be handled rather easily in Japan. A driver from Max's company picked up Gloria at the dentist's office in a company car. Max, now chugging along on the bullet train somewhere around Nagoya, had the keys to that car snugly in his pocket. All the driver had to do was merely get the model and registration number from Max's car, get the Toyota dealer to meet him with a set of master keys, get a copy of the correct key made, and find the Danger dentist in the maze of buildings comprising Shibuya. Easy. In fact the driver had done all this while the youngest Danger was still having his teeth reamed.

Additionally, the organization that is Japan easily handled the locked apartment door situation at Homat Cornucopia. Max's secretary called the rental agency, which in turn called

144

the owner, who in turn called the superintendent of another Homat whose lock-picking abilities were renowned in the "managing *gaijin* apātos" world. The front door was unlocked by the time Gloria returned home, and the sturdy craftsman was bravely standing guard—gold teeth a-flashing—to usher Gloria to the safety of her hearth. Easy.

What *is* difficult in Japan, however, is something that is relatively simple elsewhere—satisfying the demands of bureaucracy. As a result of the accident, Gloria spent the better part of the next three weeks in the following endeavors:

- Completing insurance claim forms.
- Reporting the accident to the Shibuya corner police station.
- Reporting the accident to the main Shibuya police station.
- Obtaining insurance photographs of the damaged Honda.
- Returning to the main Shibuya police station with the photographs.
- Obtaining insurance photographs—from various companies—of all damaged cars in the accident.
- Returning again to the main Shibuya police station with all the photographs.
- Completing additional insurance claim forms because the middle-aged hippie intellectual submitted medical examination bills from his "private" consultant in excess of ¥100,000. (No injury was detected.)
- Rounding up the four other drivers for a group session at the main Shibuya police station—even though there were no personal injuries, the size of the intellectual's bill raised the procedings to a new plateau of statistical intensity.
- Rescheduling the main Shibuya police station group

session when all but the intellectual showed up for the first conclave.

- Writing a note of apology to the wife of the car number one driver (who supported Gloria's testimony to the police about the lemon-yellow taxi) explaining that in her dazed condition, she mistakenly thought she saw a woman in that man's car and naturally assumed it could be none other than his wife.
- Composing three *gomen nasai* letters to officialdom for wreaking havoc in the middle of the Shibuya main intersection.
- Explaining to Max that in reality, car number one should have kept going instead of stopping since he had already missed the taxi when he slammed on his brakes. (Max believed her.)

Ironically, a few weeks later the National Azabu telephone pole attacked the repaired Honda. The parking lot attendant, who was watching, told Gloria that she should report the dented scrape to her insurance company. (Gloria didn't, and Max hasn't noticed.)

A Certain Uneasiness

"THE WISE MAN recognizes, and deals with, uneasiness as a condition of life. The fool ignores it."—Soren Kierkegaard (1813–1855) in a letter to his butcher, Hans.

MAX DANGER, nobody's fool, was too busy each day to

dwell upon the gray clouds of uneasiness that occasionally swept across the sky to the horizons of his consciousness. There were just too many specific concerns to occupy the mind. ("Danger-san, your six-ton shipment of soap flakes from the States has been impounded by Osaka customs because there is some question about the claimed purity quotient of 99 and $\frac{44}{100}$%." Or, "Daddy, when the man from the American Club visits your office, tell him we didn't know it was wrong to ride bicycles in the lobby.")

But during the quiet moments at night before sleep, Max periodically reviewed the sources of his uneasiness. They were more persistent than the specific concerns.

Why are the powerful Military Armed Forces of the United States, if one is to believe the Far East Network, peopled by souls who must be tutored on the intricacies of making out personal checks? ("And remember, you must have as much money in the bank as the number you write on the check.")

Further, is it really necessary to explain that it's probably not a good idea to shoot off rockets or help land military aircraft on the lurching decks of ships whilst stoned? ("Hey man, I've cleaned up my act and from now on I'm gonna actually pay attention to what I'm doin'.") Lord save us.

When did stealing from a base exchange, or going A.W. O.L., become a matter of "permanent entry in military records" instead of 90 days in the slammer? (It may still be, but that ain't the public impression. "C'mon all you guys and gals out there, get your heads on straight. Okay. Wow. Dig it. Now let's listen to Twisted Sister—.")

Speaking of F.E.N., aren't they supposed to interrupt their rhythmical noise with life-saving information in the event of a disaster? Three inches of snow one spring knocked them off the air! (It was during "condition white," whatever that means. Won't be able to go "TDY," whatever

147

that means. Particularly if you're "non-essential"—and we know what that means.)

In the Japanese arena, can all those "Safety in Disaster" plans really work? Imagine a levelled Tokyo—the earth still rocking and rolling, and a mass of people equivalent to a Saturday in Ginza all going in different directions. You have a question. "Excuse me, my good fellow, I wonder if you would be so kind as to point out to me where Roppongi used to be?" Will anyone remember English?

Think of the tall buildings. Architects and construction companies maintain that they are earthquake-proof. The *gomen nasai* letter, like the Confessional for Catholics, may be the ultimate face-saving (soul-saving) device employed by those architects and contractors still around after the "unfortunate miscalculations" are uncovered. ("We will try our best next time.")

And the evacuation centers? Located in "open" public areas like parks and shrines, these places are usually packed with people on Sunday afternoons—as much as eight or nine percent of the neighborhood population. Picture 90 percent of the neighborhood population in these areas. ("Excuse me, sir, I wonder if you, your friends, your relatives, and your associates might refrain from standing on the heads of my family members whilst we prepare for bed up against this tree?")

What bothered Max more—made him increasingly uneasy—was in the area of free trade and balanced economies. What if the Japanese markets open—*really* open? What if the lobbyists, trade associations, bureaucrats, and politicians say "to hell with it—we want all the foreign goods we can possibly lay our hands on?" The foreign businessmen would have to deliver. No excuses. Hmm.

What if several American companies, for example, *actually* delivered. Imagine every Honda and Toyota in Japan

148

replaced by a Chevrolet Bel Air and a Ford LTD. The Shuto would go to one lane, and the parking space in Tokyo by Max's estimate, would be reduced by 17.5 percent. Fuel costs would approach rental expense in the expat package. Western foreigners, in order to avoid being tabbed by the local populace as being "American," would have to remain hiding indoors during periods of "recall." ("All General Motors cars produced this decade must be returned immediately to the dealer as the front wheels have a tendency to fall off.")

Contemplate foreign corporations suddenly doubling their Japan expectations. Great. That's a lot of merchandise and more jobs back home. Acme Electronics of Akron would go from two to four expats in Tokyo.

But remember IBM. Where would the rest of us live? Ken Corporation and Sun Realty would be opening branches in Niigata. ("The public school system in Nagaoka is actually quite good, and a number of people up there have actually *seen* foreigners before. The commute is a little rough, though.") The Oriental Bazaar would take over the lower third of Omote Sando, and begin supplementing Japanese "antiques" with pottery purchased wholesale in San Francisco. Are we ready for this? Max asked himself.

Despite all of the above, there was one source of uneasiness that haunted Max more than others as he dropped off to sleep at night. It was something he had not really verbalized, although he suspected the beautiful Gloria was having similar thoughts on the subject. Max had even overheard the kids talking about it with their school chums.

Here they were—*gaijin,* aliens, outsiders—in a decidedly foreign country. Mastery of the language formed with age a perversely inverse ratio to accomplishment. (Max's youngest usually ordered dinner for the family and got them home in the taxi.)

But the uneasiness would have to be dealt with as a specific concern before too many years went by. It was beginning to make Max re-evaluate his programmed career path as defined by his corporate leaders.

The international schools in Japan *are* good. The beautiful Gloria was involved in things unheard of in suburban U.S.A. Max was beginning to understand how to zap things through the countless staff meetings. Despite the prices, there was money in the bank.

What if, only *if* mind you, the family really wanted to stay in Japan—beyond the terms of the corporate assignment for example? One could do a whole lot worse. And in many respects, not a whole lot better.

The Case of the Horrible Misunderstanding,
or
Here Comes Miss Fujii Again

FAITHFUL READERS of the Danger adventures will recall that early in the Tokyo Assignment, Max fell prey—albeit temporarily and inconclusively—to the charms and wiles of a local young lovely.

Miss Fujii, bank teller extraordinaire, had once been for Max an object of reverie in idle moments and a subject of speculative titillation during actual check-cashing moments. Almond-shaped eyes, moist lips, luxuriant black hair framing a perfectly oval face, and a marvelously tidy little body were combined with a penetrating appreciation of subtle wit and humor. (Miss Fujii's pert little self nearly fell off her bank teller's stool in hysterics when Max once replied that he wanted his cash in ¥20,000 notes.)

Max and Miss Fujii, you'll remember, went out dining and dancing one evening after work. Miss Fujii's avowed interest was "getting to know foreigner with good spirit." Max's interest was unavowed, but suffice to say it was rooted in the "wonder what it's like" syndrome that frequently visits Westerners new to the Orient. (It was less, Max rationalized, a matter of moral ambivalence than it was a manifestation of the same quest for adventure that sends explorers to strange and uncharted worlds.)

The evening had ended, after a series of cultural, perceptual, and generational misunderstandings, with both parties remaining resolutely chaste. It's just as well—life is complicated enough as it is.

Max did the right thing by Miss Fujii, however. He introduced her to a Young Foreigner of his acquaintance who parted his blond hair near the middle, and wore striped ties and old fashioned shoes. Most importantly, he was a bachelor. His "good spirit" was just itching to be "known" by the likes of Miss Fujii. It was a match made, if not in heaven, then certainly in the secular temples of unattached singles. The Young Foreigner and Miss Fujii became regulars at many of the Roppongi "in" places.

Alas, Gentle Reader, life *is* complicated. It can be a very small world out there. The Young Foreigner, whose "good spirit" perhaps exceeded Miss Fujii's capacity to "know," expanded his activities. He expanded them right into Max's office. He also began to date one of Max's clerk-typists, the innocent Miss Inose. The Young Foreigner was, as they say, "dividing his time." He and Miss Inose also became regulars at many of the Roppongi "in" places. Not the same nights as with Miss Fujii, of course.

Why, you ask, is this turn of events relevant? The fact

that Max spent a moderately delightful evening once with Miss Fujii, who later became involved with the Young Foreigner, who in turn was now hitting upon a Danger employee, is certainly nothing to be concerned about. We're all adults.

Well, the day of the Horrible Misunderstanding demonstrated that Max's vague misgivings about things were well-founded. Looking back on it now, Max readily admits that the situation could be interpreted as being mildly amusing. However, for a while there, it was touch and go.

Max invariably arrived in the office at 9:04 in the morning. It made no difference when he got out of bed—knots in his pajama strings, dull razors, Paul Harvey, and traffic all conspired to maintain that tardy consistency.

The staff would always be in the middle of the "morning meeting" when he walked in. No one paid particular attention to him—the regularity and predictability of his appearance was probably a comfortable element in the daily routine.

On the day of the Horrible Misunderstanding, Max made his normal entrance. He had not taken two steps beyond the outer doors when he realized something was terribly wrong. Sixty-one pairs of brown eyes—considerably wider than normal—were looking at him. Serious Hirose, who had been conducting the meeting, stopped in mid-exhortation.

The door to Max's private office, behind his secretary's desk, was closed. (He had never seen it closed before, at least from the outside.) His secretary, usually an island of passive tranquility in all storms at sea, glowered. Wailing, which Max now noticed, was coming from behind the door.

When in doubt, Max's grandfather once advised, stride with confidence. Max strode confidentally to the door and opened it. (Max's grandfather was frequently wrong.)

152

"MAX, I WANT YOU—"

Max stepped inside and closed the door.

"— to tell me which girl is Inose."

There writhed Miss Fujii, bank teller extraordinaire, considerably disheveled. She was rocking back and forth on Max's midget couch—tears, traced with mascara, made long lines down her perfectly oval face. Her hair looked knotted. She had taken her shoes off and was nervously and repeatedly undoing and fastening the top two or three buttons of her blouse. Her normally moist lips were dry and cracked. Her entrance to his office, Max reflected, must have been spectacular.

"What are you doing here?" soothed Max.

"Which one is she?"

"Why do you want to know?" asked Max, instantly regretting the question.

"BECAUSE I KILL HER—" (Max's secretary had opened the door and asked about tea or coffee)"—that's why," continued Miss Fujii as the door slammed shut.

"Maybe you should talk about this with the Young Foreigner," suggested Max.

"He's away in Singapore on business trip," Miss Fujii screeched.

"I am *really* sorry to hear that," Max said with feeling. He suddenly wondered what it would feel like to strangle a man wearing a 100 percent cotton button-down dress shirt.

"And when he comes back," Miss Fujii continued, "he will marry that Inose of yours."

"Goodness," said Max.

"But I want to see her first and tell her truth about him."

"That's not a good idea, why not—"

"AND THEN I KILL HER." (Max's secretary had returned with coffee.)

153

It took about an hour for Miss Fujii to calm down. Max's sympathies were with her, but his responsibilities were to his employees. He did not produce the innocent Miss Inose. But he did promise to arrange a meeting between the Young Foreigner and Miss Fujii as soon as the cad returned from hiding. Miss Fujii was grateful.

It was just as Miss Fujii impulsively kissed Max on the cheek for his "understanding" that his secretary entered with an announcement about visitors in the lobby. As luck would have it, the top of the blouse was in the "unbuttoned" stage.

"Ah, er, Miss Fujii will be leaving now," he reported.

"Good," replied Max's secretary, "because you must call back your wife before seeing visitors." She thoughtfully repeated the instruction in Japanese.

In a way, the story has a happy ending. The Young Foreigner and the innocent Miss Inose eventually married. Miss Fujii pined for a week or two, but has since been seen around the Roppongi "in" places with another foreigner whose "spirit" is no doubt "good."

Circumstances trapped Max, however. Later in the evening on the day of the Horrible Misunderstanding, the Young Foreigner had called his bride-to-be, the innocent Miss Inose, from Singapore. They discussed, as lovers do, this and that. They probably made plans for the wedding. Miss Inose had exciting news to tell.

"Someone named Fujii came to our office today."

"Oh?" replied the Young Foreigner. (He later told Max that he felt his entrails freezing at that precise moment.)

"And we're not sure, but we think it must be our boss Danger-san's mistress." (His entrails at that moment, he also told Max, thawed.)

"What do you think?" asked the innocent Miss Inose.

The Young Foreigner was never able to report his answer in Max's presence. (It's difficult to speak when your striped tie is radically tightened around the collar of your 100 percent cotton button-down dress shirt.)

Max was not invited to the wedding. In fact, the Young Foreigner tends to leave the room now whenever Max enters.

Explaining Things Clearly

EFFECTIVE COMMUNICATION is often taken for granted. We humans have evolved a marvelous system whereby our throats and mouths—in close coordination with our tongues and teeth—emit a variety of sounds which, because of an ability to duplicate and repeat these sounds in connection with recognizable behavior patterns, make our innermost thoughts and intentions crystal clear.

Many living creatures, we are told, communicate within their species. In the lower orders of life, the transfer of information is admittedly limited to the needs of the moment. Fish, for example, are rarely called upon to describe to their households the intricacies involved with setting digital watches. Fish don't wear digital watches.

Yet fish somehow get the idea across to friends and relatives that it's a better idea to swim upstream to spawn than downstream. Birds, bees, and rhinoceri are equally clever at getting points across to others within their species. Some creatures are very clever indeed. Witness the swallows at Capistrano. Consider bankers when the trust markets open.

155

Humans, however, bear a special burden in communicating effectively. Not only is our subject matter often more complex than standard rabbit chatter, our abilities to modify sounds issuing from our throats have led us off into a multitude of "variations" which we call "languages."

What is one man's *"la plume"* becomes another man's *"enpitsu,"* when in fact the thing that leaks ink on the fingers is clearly a "ball point pen." It's a shame not everyone appreciates this—life would be simpler if *they* called things by their correct names.

Max Danger, it goes without saying, had "hit the wall" in the communication category on any number of occasions during the Tokyo assignment. The combination of a determined effort to master basic words and phrases, plus a willingness to try them in any and all circumstances, was beginning to pay off, however.

His throat and mouth, in close coordination with his tongue and teeth, were gradually duplicating more and more sounds leading to predictable behavior on the part of communicatees. They were peculiar sounds, of course, but they worked.

There were, nevertheless, spectacular setbacks.

Max bought the beautiful Gloria a wristwatch for her birthday. It may have been the most sensible gift he'd ever given his wife—it certainly seemed to cause a more positive reaction than the bicycle he'd given her the year before, or for that matter, the banjo the year before that.

That presentation of the wristwatch was made during a family dinner at a moderately classy Japanese restaurant. The Danger family had a private room, sat on tatami, and "pigged out" on shabu-shabu. Everyone had fun, and the watch was a hit.

It didn't fit, however. The metal band was too tight on Gloria's wrist. Upon examination all agreed that the band was probably adjustable, but all equally agreed that Max would certainly break it if he tried to adjust it. In fact, all agreed, it may need an extra link.

"No problem," said Max. "I'll take the watch back to the store for adjustment."

"No problem," everyone concluded. "Isn't the food good?"

"And the restaurant nice."

"And our legs sore."

"How will you know," asked the level-headed Danger daughter, "how big to make the band without Mommy's wrist with you in the store?"

Everyone laughed—a family laugh—but the question had merit. After discussion, a solution was agreed upon. Max, using a fancy shoelace from the youngster's tennis shoe, measured the precise circumference of the beautiful Gloria's wrist. ("Oh my, aren't we having fun at Mommy's birthday party.") He tied a knot in the shoelace, indicating the measurement, about a quarter of the way along the length of the string.

"No problem," everyone said again.

"No problem," Max agreed.

He returned to the watch store the following day, shoelace in hand. It should be mentioned that the store, although located at the edge of Ginza, was decidedly off the path normally beaten by *gaijin* shoppers. Down a narrow side street, one would have to be either looking for that exact store or be lost to discover it. (Max had been lost.)

The sales force—two giggling girls and a near-sighted older gentleman—had been somewhat flustered when Max originally appeared, lost, and made his purchase. Dealing with foreigners was clearly not part of the normal routine of that store's personnel.

Max's return, waving the shoelace, elevated the fluster-level to a seven-point-five on the open-ended Japanese scale.

His throat and mouth, in close coordination with his tongue and teeth, emitted sounds. They were matched and modified by the giggling girls and the near-sighted gentleman.

"More *okii,"* Max explained, spreading his hands wide. He demonstrated with the shoelace on the wrist of one of the gigglers. He pointed to the knot. He demonstrated again on the thick wrist of the gentleman. *"Dame,"* Max said expressing displeasure with the fit. The gentleman peered intently at the knot. Max repeated the routine. He concluded the charade with the approximation of the sounds meaning "foreigners are very big."

A great deal of conversation ensued amongst the members of the sales force. One of the gigglers seemed to grasp the situation, and Max expressed agreement with her analysis. It was suggested that Max return the following day to pick up the adjusted wristwatch. Sounds meaning "foreigners are very big" followed Max as he was bowed out of the store.

When he did pick up the adjusted wristwatch, Max was mildly surprised to note that the salesforce had grown to include a matronly lady and a high school-aged boy. There was barely room for all of them behind the counter. Max was given the box containing the watch, and it was pointed out to him that the knotted shoelace was in a separate little package. The boy said, "I hope okay," in English. Max thanked them all profusely as he backed from the store. Two workers from a *ramen* shop across the narrow street stared at him. Max smiled and gave them a slight nod.

The presentation of the adjusted wristwatch to Gloria at dinner that night may well go down in Danger family lore for generations to come. In presenting the box containing the watch to Gloria, Max pointed out to the children the importance of studying languages. "Otherwise," he said, "how can situations like this be effectively handled?"

The oldest Danger offspring later reported that he firmly believed he was going "to die laughing"—in fact, for a few moments there, he said, he could not breathe, and probably even "blacked out."

The middle child immediately called her girlfriends once she regained her composure, and she and they remained on the phone laughing most of the evening.

The youngest child wet his pants (and for once did not break into tears).

Gloria hugged Max.

The watch store had adjusted the watchband—adding links—to the exact millimeter from the knot in the shoelace to the end of the string. The wrong end.

The beautiful Gloria could slip her new wristwatch over her head and wear it around her neck.

The Team

MAX DANGER recognized the "superlative degree principle," and understood its effects, early in his grade school days. In any group, someone is always going to be the smartest, dumbest, prettiest, luckiest, craziest, healthiest or sickest. Adam and Eve probably discussed this phenomenon.

The dynamics of group interaction reinforces expectations, so that by the time one reaches puberty, like it or not, a pattern of behavior is established.

The smart kid believes it of himself and does well in subsequent academic pursuits. The sick kid becomes a doctor, jogs, and doesn't smoke. The dumb kid becomes a plumber and earns more than the doctor. The pretty kid believes until senility that her "aura" dominates all relationships. The crazy kid becomes a currency trader.

Max, of course, had a superlative category. Whilst it was significant in boyhood, it was of absolutely no importance or relevance to anything since. (Even the fat kid became a middle linebacker and earned a Super Bowl ring.)

Max could run, from the front door of his classroom to the tree in the corner of the playground, faster than anyone in the school. By high school, he could run the equivalent distance faster than anyone in his part of the country. By college, faster than all but a few dozen folks on this planet. But unless one goes in for cheetah-chasing or street-mugging, the talent develops nothing in the way of adult career possibilities.

So while the dumb kid was building condos in Florida with earnings from the plumbing trade, the sick kid was snorting ether and advising rich patients on the thrills of sobriety, and the smart kid was collecting corporate stock options, Max was standing in short pants—middle-age bulge distorting the waistband—at the starting line of a 100 meter dash final in the Japan National Stadium at Yoyogi on a grey, chilly, wind-swept afternoon in October. He was older, by at least a decade, than anyone but the coaches in the stadium.

A black shot-putter from Yokota and Max were the only *gaijin* to reach the finals. Winners were scheduled to represent Japan in the Asian Games to be held in Manila. Even having *gaijin* in the finals appeared to be generating consternation on the part of the officials, but it was an "open" meet and there was little that could be done about it.

Enough *was* done, however, to the black shot putter. He was disqualified on a "form" technicality during his final toss. Nothing can be done, meanwhile, about one who can dash to the tree in the corner of the playground faster than anybody. Max won his event, and made the "Japanese" team.

It was midway through the series of practice sessions for the Manila trip that Max observed the crumbling of the "superlative degree principle"—at least as it applies to Japanese athletics. Naturally, everyone was measured and outfitted with identical warm-up suits, track outfits, and even white sport coats with little rising suns on the breast pockets. After several negotiations, Max was granted the right to wear his own track shoes—only if they were white. (His were fifteen years old, not nifty, and black.) He gave in, but then white shoes could not be found that fit. More consternation. An "exception" was made, and the black shoes were "approved."

But it was during the actual workouts that he saw the principle crumble. All the exercises for all the participants in all the events were done altogether. Max had never seen a discus thrower run more than five meters. He had never seen a shot putter even run. Ten thousand-meter entrants practiced starts with the sprinters and high jumpers. Hours were spent by everyone either on the ground, or against poles, stretching.

Max jogged with the group—jogging builds "wind" and endurance. It was the first time he had ever jogged. Sprinters only take three or four breaths during a race, and endurance is not even a factor. Either a dash man is able to explode with power at the start, keep the feet snapping in front of a

161

forward-leaning body, and push hard, into the finish—or he is not. Jogging from here to Spain won't help. Max wondered what the discus thrower chugging along next to him was thinking.

Clearly, no one was paying attention to the "superlative degree principle." The strongest guys were not particularly asked to be strong, the quickest guys were not particularly working on quickness, leapers were not particularly leaping. The training was designed to build a "team," as if the parts were interchangeable. If the names of all participants in an international track meet were to be drawn from a hat, and people were to be assigned to events at random, Japan would win hands down. Everybody was more or less conditioned to do everything.

The trip to Manila was an exercise in togetherness. Max, in his white sport coat with a rising sun, attracted considerable attention. He explained, to anyone who asked, that he was an *ainu*.

His seat companion on the flight was a pole vaulter. They were teammates. They discussed grips and the material composition of poles. During twenty years of competitive running, on several different continents, Max had never even *spoken* to a pole vaulter, let alone considered one a teammate. He actually began to worry about whether or not the man had his grips right.

The track meet itself went as all do—hours of boredom interspersed with moments of frantic activity. The Japanese team began piling up points early, if for no other reason than the sheer numbers of entries it had in each event.

Max separated himself from the group and hung around with the other sprinters as they worked their way through the heats. The atmosphere of near savage intensity and highly concentrated emotion that dash men must develop in order to burst into immediate full stride was familiar and oddly comforting. (Max once saw a West German punch a Canadian and knock him unconscious because the Canadian walked in front of the German as they were readying for a sprint. The German, quite honestly, could not remember doing it.)

Max made the finals. As he was preparing for the last race, a corner of his consciousness noticed teammates cheering for him. That, as far as he could remember, was a first.

The eight-lane start was mediocre. Within nine or ten strides, the muscular kid from the Philippines wearing brown dress socks had edged out in front. At 40 meters a guy with thick thighs from Jakarta pulled even. He was grunting rhythmically.

Someone screamed behind Max, a popped tendon no doubt. ("There, but for the grace of God—") Max could feel the black guy from Fiji in the next lane, but couldn't see him. Max's right hamstring was tightening. Timers shouted something at 60 meters. Max's eyes crossed, as they usually did, at about at about 75 meters. He could no longer feel the Fijian.

The lean began for the tape. Someone broke wind. Max clipped the guy from Jakarta at the finish, but placed second to the Filipino by about a stride. Someone threw up on his heels as they all trotted down. The Filipino, who was now the fastest to the tree in the playground, took a lap with his arms in the air. Good for him.

What Max remembered most, however—other than the fact that it had been his second slowest time since college—was the cheering of his teammates. The best-dressed group of athletes in the stadium surrounded and congratulated him. The discus thrower, who had chugged along next to Max on their interminable practice jogs, led the group.

All the way back to Tokyo on the plane, the team

reveled in its triumphs, laughed at its misfortunes. (The long-jumper scratched on each and every attempt, the 400 meter relay team—of which Max had been a part—set an Asian Games record.)

In all of Max's previous experiences, the "superlative degree principle" meant that individuals privately raged or privately rejoiced at the accidents of achievement. (He once considered, albeit momentarily, jumping *out* of a plane returning from Europe after he had accidentally and briefly run out of his lane on the curve during a relay race—thereby disqualifying his foursome. No one had spoken to him during that entire journey home.)

But Max's new colleagues were only interested in the performance of the whole team as a group. Individuals merely had to "do their best." The long-jumper probably had more beer poured for him than any other person on the squad. Sinking into the group, with its support and shared excitement, was genuinely fun and certainly comfortable. Max the *ainu* sang "Jingle Bells" in Japanese and kissed the stewardesses. His behavior for the situation was normal.

The team broke up at Narita. It never will, or never could be, exactly the same—at least for Max. He concluded, during the long taxi ride to Azabu, that you may beat them as individuals, but you'll play hell beating them as a group. Max has not worn the track shoes since, and now wonders if the smartest kid back home is lonely.

Another "Only in Japan" Story

MAX DANGER's domestic administrative skills, on a scale of one to ten, approached zero.

Mind you, a great part of this was by design. Can there be a "harried" executive who *really* wants to know how to activate the Homat dishwasher, or even wants to be in the same room when the paper boy arrives to collect?

The attitude is probably sexist—relegating to a housewife the chores of the house has somehow become unfashionable in recent years. Yet the challenge involved with getting a plumber to come and fix the master bedroom toilet matches or exceeds the challenge involved with staying awake during a Japanese sales presentation in the office. And it is certainly more satisfying.

The beautiful Gloria, mother of three and PTA member at three different schools, had the Danger household affairs in excellent order. Things worked. Max appreciated the probable complexity of the systems, but was blithely ignorant of any and all details.

Difficulties arose, therefore, during Max's first period of sustained bachelorhood in Japan. Gloria, with the kids, went on Home Leave a month before Max. He was given written instructions. They were taped to the refrigerator door next to the "Far Side" cartoons. Nevertheless, the systems broke down.

Watering the plants was easy. Despite the instructions, it

was not necessary to do it every third day. A big dose of water on Saturday mornings sufficed. A lot of leaves fell off, but the ones remaining were more or less green. As a point of interest, plants do not thrive on Kirin Light Beer. The specific plants participating in that Noble Experiment had to be replaced.

Bringing the damn cat to the vet for shots was *not* so easy. Max couldn't understand Gloria's map. He and the damn cat wandered around Azabu Juban for three straight weekends looking for the vet. They never found him. Cats *do* thrive on Kirin Light Beer, however. Max deemed the shots unnecessary.

It may be interesting to know that two cups of clothes washing soap, when introduced into the dishwasher, produce sufficient foam to cover a Homat kitchen floor to the depth of an average man's shins. It may also be interesting to learn that refrigerator machinery stops working when it's befouled by foam.

Max's dishwashing problems were solved brilliantly, however, when it occurred to him to stack the dirty dishes in the bathtub. He, and they, showered together each morning.

Another chore assigned to Max was to take the garbage out regularly. The assignment was perhaps the simplest of all. It merely meant depositing trash outside the apartment door. He remembered to do this every half–dozen days or so, whenever the empty Campbell's soup cans could no longer be stacked on the empty Kirin Light Beer cans.

But the "Only In Japan" experience involved Max's dress shirts. Gloria's notes were uncharacteristically silent on the matter.

Max *did* know that twice a week he would get his shirts ready for the laundry. Getting them ready meant putting them in an empty National Azabu Supermarket bag and giving the bag to Gloria. Gloria had arranged for someone to pick them up, wash and starch them, and deliver them a few days later.

How, and particularly when, this ritual took place was in detail a mystery to Max. After about a week of piling up dirty shirts, Max realized he was approaching the bottom of the clean shirt stack. Within a few more days, he was prompted to act.

Max put the shirts in a National Azabu Supermarket bag. He put the bag outside his door. It was a long, long time before he saw the shirts again.

Most *gaijin* cannot buy ready-made shirts in Japan. If the neck fits, then the body of the shirt contemplates draping a sumotori. If the shoulders fit, then the sleeves stop at the elbows. Etc.

Hotels do have one-day laundry service, however. The price is moderate—only about one third the cost of a new shirt. Max found himself rotating his three remaining dress shirts through the Hotel Okura facilities whilst awaiting the clean shirts from Gloria's laundry. He visited the hotel on behalf of his remaining shirts every other day for two-and-a-half weeks. He was approaching, in expenses, the cost of an airplane ticket to Korea where cheap shirts that fit are thrown at people.

Collars, and tempers, were beginning to fray when word of his shirts' fate finally reached Max. His secretary, of all people, received a call—in the office. It was from the laundry that handled the "Danger account." His shirts had had quite an adventure. But think of the organization that is Japan.

Max's shirts had been collected by the garbage men. They were nice shirts, mind you, but garbage men have a lot to do as they scurry on their rounds. They can't be expected to review the contents of each bag they pick up.

The shirts went for a ride on one of those little blue garbage trucks. It was probably nice and warm back in there with the grapefruit rinds, fish heads, and yakitori orts.

The shirts spent the next few days out around Harumi somewhere at a district collection center. There they were joined by Shibuya banana peels and Chiyoda curries.

Garbage, at a district collection center, is sorted by brave men in hip boots using rakes and shovels. (Max later went out and watched them.) The technique employed is to break open garbage bags by slamming the back of the rake against the bags, thereby splitting them open. Then the trash is roughly sorted into piles.

The distinction in piles has something to do with how well the material will burn. The various piles are shovelled on to skids and trundled off to three different types of incinerators.

The result of the exercise is compacted matter that is then used for land-fill. At the current rate of garbage accumulation, the Japanese will be able to walk to Hawaii 100 years from now.

Somewhere along the way, in one of the sorting phases, Max's shirts made their appearance. It is interesting to consider what must have gone on in the head of the man in hip boots. He probably poked them around a bit with his rake. He must have picked one up and looked at it closely. He probably noticed the National Azabu Supermarket bag. He most certainly saw "Danger" written in katakana on the inside collar. He probably leaned on his rake, lit a cigarette, and stared at the shirts for a while. He finally reported the matter to his supervisor.

The various Kanto laundry associations were contacted. (There are seven or eight.) A circular was distributed, and Everest Laundry of Roppongi responded affirmatively. They had a "Danger" account.

168

The Homat Cornucopia janitor was contacted. (No one was home during the day in the Danger apartment.) The janitor had no idea where Max worked, but he remembered seeing Tokyo American Club parking stickers on the Danger vehicles. The club was notified, and put the laundry in contact with Max's secretary. The problem was solved. Max got his shirts. Only in Japan.

But the real touch—the quintessence of subtlety that characterizes this society—was the condition of the washed and starched shirts. Clearly, the shirts had had a rough go. There were probably cabbage leaves in the pockets and rake marks on the sleeves. Associated odors were best left to imagination.

Max's favorite shirt, a blue-and-white striped devil, had been missing the second (but not first) cuff button for several months. Gloria had not gotten around to sewing on a replacement. That had been mildly disconcerting to Max.

The shirts were delivered to the Danger apartment. They were as clean and fresh as they'd ever been. Someone had sewn a second cuff button on the striped shirt.

The Brooklyn Fire Costume Affair

IN THE GOOD old days, expat warriors were sent abroad to do battle with local customs and heathen habits armed only with Christian bibles, Royal Sanctions, a sense of mission, and repeat-action rifles. The challenges were clear—"Do what you can to bring *them* around to our way of thinking."

Independent decisions were necessarily based upon the needs of the moment. ("We'll return the fertile but sacred burial grounds provided you don't eat my wife and children.") Issues were unambiguous.

Head Office communication, in the good old days, was sporadic at best. With luck, one could manage the assignment with only one or two pieces of advice "from home" every decade.

Modern times changed all that. Old China Hands, for example, tell stories about working frantically whenever the mail boat managed to flounder into port. It would be one week of intense activity—answering correspondence and filing invoices—then a blessedly indeterminant amount of time for "market research" and gin. What a shock it must have been when the boats began showing up on a more or less regular basis every two or three months. ("Will a man ever he able to pull it all together?") Contemplative time was compressed.

Telegraph machinery, and the attendant wires and cables, virtually destroyed the leisure of contemplation. Real answers, of all things, were required within 24 to 48 hours. (Historians record that it was during this phase of expat existence that the sentence, "Please re-transmit, message garbled," was invented.) Sometimes two, even three, things piled up on the desk at once.

Telephones, the curse of mankind, completely obliterated contemplative thought. Words and phrases supplanted ideas, and expathood was forever changed. (Facsimile tomfoolery, an evil offspring of the phone business, merely exacerbates the problem. Computer terminals are too painful even to discuss.)

The point of all this—the circumstantial horror facing expats today—is that authority back home mistakes the speed

170

of data transmission with knowledge. *They think they know as much as we do!*

Furthermore, armed with the bogus equation of "knowledge," *they* advise *us* on local matters. ("Tell the Ministry of Finance that our corporate vice-president will not approve your plan—Japan must instead re-structure its licensing procedures, preferably by Thursday.") The technology of communicating is destroying communication.

Max Danger's experience in this regard was epitomized by "The Brooklyn Fire Costume Affair." His company, an American-based international conglomerate, employed all the latest technology. Data transmission is instant. Each exchange of words and phrases, however, raised the bewilderment quotient to new and ecstatically high levels of perplexity. The following occurred over a period of six working days.

To Max: "AT 10:18 TODAY BOARD APPROVED ACQUISITION OF BROOKLYN FIRE. BY 11:40 INVESTMENT DEPT REPORTS 43.2 PCT STOCK OWNERSHIP. PLSE PREPARE SALES CAMPAIGN REMAINDER THIS YEAR PLUS FIVE-YEAR PROJECTION AND SUBMIT BY END OF WEEK."

To Head Office: "CONGRATULATIONS AND BEST WISHES. IS BROOKLYN FIRE AN INSURANCE COMPANY?"

To Max: "NOT FUNNY. PLSE REFER TRANSMISSION 43-7451A (AMENDED MARCH) FOR DETAILS. INCLUDE CONTINGENT CAMPAIGN COSTS IN REPORT."

To Head Office: "UNHAVE MARCH VERSION 43-7451A. HAVE ONLY REFERENCE TO KANSAS CITY FAST FOOD/FERTILIZER MERGER."

171

To Max: "IT WAS TRANSMITTED MAY 5."

To Head Office: "OF TRANSMISSIONS LOGGED MAY 6 (YOUR TIME MAY 5) NOTHING ON BROOKLYN FIRE. IS IT INSURANCE COMPANY?"

To Max: "YOUR RELUCTANCE TO COOPERATE NOTED. BROOKLYN FIRE MAJOR MANUFACTURER FIRE SAFETY APPAREL. REPORT DUE FRIDAY."

To Head Office: "APPRECIATE REPORT DUE FRIDAY BUT PLSE DESCRIBE DETAILS OF PRODUCT."

To Max: "BROOKLYN FIRE COSTUME OLDEST CONTINUOUS FIRM THIS TYPE IN USA. WE NOW OWN, AS OF 13:16, TOTAL 62.8 PCT COMMON STOCK AND HAVE ACQUIRED OPTIONS ON 28 PCT PREFERRED. PRICE NOW (13:18) TRADING 47 OVER THE COUNTER. STATE ESTIMATED SALES FIGURES IN DOLLARS."

To Head Office: "ABSOLUTELY THRILLED OVER DETAILS OF STOCK DEAL. DO PEOPLE ENDURING OR PEOPLE FIGHTING FIRES WEAR THESE COSTUMES?"

To Max: "SUGGEST YOUR INITIAL CONTACT BE TOKYO FIRE CHIEF OR EQUIVALENT. HOWEVER WE NEEDN'T REMIND YOU THAT IS YOUR JOB TO ORGANIZE. WE CANNOT DO EVERYTHING FROM HERE. SEPARATE ACTUAL FROM ANTICIPATED ORDERS IN YOUR REPORT."

To Head Office: "DO FIRE COSTUMES HAVE POINTY HATS AND SILVER BUCKLES ON SHOES?"

To Max: SPECIFICATION DETAIL UNKNOWN THIS

DEPT. AM REFERRING YOUR QUERY TO ENGINEERING. STOCK NOW TRADING 61. WASHINGTON WONDERS IF DIFFICULTIES WE EXPERIENCING THIS PRODUCT SHOULD BE INCLUDED IN U.S.–JAPAN TRADE STUDY REPORT? REPLY IMMEDIATELY ALONG WITH REPORT DUE TODAY."

To Head Office: "FLOODING IN TYPING POOL NOW UNDER CONTROL BUT OUR REPORT DELAYED WHILST RUBBLE CLEARED AND CHOLERA SHOTS ADMINISTERED. SUGGEST BROOKLYN FIRE COSTUME SITUATION NOT, REPEAT NOT, BE INCLUDED U.S.–JAPAN TRADE STUDY REPORT DUE TO ONGOING DELICATE NEGOTIATIONS. DO THESE THINGS COME IN SMALL SIZE?"

To Max: "STOCK THIS MOMENT (15:37) BROKE 70."

To Head Office: "WE ALL FLABBERGASTED YOUR SUCCESSES. COSTUMES NOT MADE OF PAPER ARE THEY?"

To Max: "URGENT. IMMEDIATELY CEASE ALL NEGOTIATIONS BROOKLYN FIRE. CANCEL CONTRACTS AND REFER PENALTY DAMAGES TO HEAD OFFICE LEGAL DEPT. BROOKLYN FIRE DIVESTED."

Max closed his file. He did re-open it briefly several weeks later to enter the report from the Engineering Department. The shoes were really boots, and the buckles were a metal alloy, not silver. No mention was made of the shape of the hats.

Pals

THE KID had a good arm. He was skinny, wore thick wire-rimmed glasses, and ran on his heels.

His legs, hanging down from short pants, were unusually thin. His knees were wider than his thighs.

He was a solemn youngster, very pale, and looked to be ten or eleven. Max noticed him the day the Dangers moved into Homat Cornucopia. He was flinging a rubber "baseball" against the side of the apartment building. (If the rebound was low, he tended to turn his head as he scooped the ball from the pavement.)

But the kid could really whip his arm. He would pause between each throw, stare at the closely-grouped ball marks on the wall, and go into his windup. His delivery was smooth, but by snapping his forearm as he released the ball, he gave it extra velocity. WHAP.

Max knew, having once been around ten or eleven himself, what was going on in the kid's head. He was pitching in the major leagues.

Max next noticed him a week or so later. The kid paused in his pitching chores as Max drove his car across "the infield" and into the Homat garage. The kid avoided Max's eyes, and instead looked at the fans in the upper deck.

After about a month of interrupting "the game," Max joined the kid. On an impulse, he walked out of the garage and back to where the kid was pitching.

174

With an ease that reflects one of the more universally accepted relationships between men, and without a word exchanged, they began a game of catch. The kid hummed the ball to Max. Max snapped it back. The kid was not particularly anxious to field grounders. Max was not particularly anxious to catch the kid's fastballs barehanded. Accommodations were made.

At precisely 6:30 P.M., a lady emerged from the house next to Homat Cornucopia and said something to the kid. Wordlessly, the kid took his ball and glove and disappeared into the house after her. Max went home, his fingers and palms stinging.

Max bought a baseball glove in Kanda. For the remainder of the fall and throughout the winter, Max and the kid whipped the ball back and forth. During the winter, they moved the game down the driveway and played "under the lights."

They played catch in the drizzling rain, with cold winds slicing down the driveway, and while snowflakes fell. They once played in three inches of slush—standing in tire tracks to keep from slipping.

The kid's name was Hiro. (Max's name was Max—ballplayers don't stand on formality.) The kid was still timid about "looking" ground balls into his glove. Probably the glasses. Max showed him how to drop to one knee to at least block ground balls and keep them from getting past him. He was eager to learn.

The kid got stronger in the spring. As much for the sake of his left palm as anything, Max showed the kid how to throw a change-up. He also showed him how to snap his wrist at the release to produce the rudiments of a curve.

As a summer began, Max noticed that the lady allowed the kid to stay out until 6:45. That was fine for the game—it allowed Max to get to the ballpark for around three

175

sessions per week. It made Max's dinners at home less comfortable, however. Hosts should never perspire into the canapes whilst passing them to guests.

The invitation arrived in mid-July. It had been slipped under the door of the Danger apartment. None of the printed matter was in English. Someone, however, had carefully inscribed in block letters a note across the top. "MY HUSBAND HAS DEAD," said the note. "THANK YOU IF YOU CAN," said the addendum at the bottom. Max took the document to his office for translation.

The invitation was to a father-son outing at Korakuen to see the Giants play the Swallows. It was sponsored by Hiro's grade school. *Obento,* the invitation reported, would be provided.

Max and the kid went. About 40 fathers and sons attended in a group. Max, of course, was the object of no little curiosity at first, but once the game began, and once the discussions relative to the merits of various players began, Max's "foreignness" was more or less forgotten. It didn't hurt to have bought the first round of Cokes and beer.

The group had good seats—they were almost immediately behind home plate. Max and the kid sat at the edge of the group's section so as to be as close as possible to a direct line from pitcher to catcher. Egawa was pitching for the Giants, and that was a bonus.

Max and the kid not only called balls and strikes as fast as the home plate umpire, they named the pitches. After a while, most of the kids drifted down to where Max and Hiro were sitting. Fathers tended to stay at the other end of the section, hitting the *obento,* and drinking beer.

Max and Hiro discussed curve balls and finger placements on sliders. It struck Max that Hiro had probably never been the center of attention with the other boys during any consideration of athletics or physical activity. The other kids

176

were roughnecks—they sported the standard bruises and scrapes.

Hiro, meanwhile, sat primly, solemn eyes blinking slowly behind his glasses, predicting every pitch before it was thrown. A couple kids whacked him on the back when he correctly predicted a low fastball ending an inning. It was a good afternoon. (The Swallows won.)

Max brought Hiro a genuine Chicago Cubs baseball cap back from Home Leave. They played catch a few more times that autumn, but Hiro's study schedule and Max's business commitments limited the games to two or three times a month.

The kid's house was torn down in a day-and-a-half. It was replaced by a "mansion." Hookers and dentists live there now.

Max and the kid played catch the day the moving trucks packed him out. The kid was wearing the Cubs cap. Max was pleased to see a large scrape on the kid's knee—he was, he said, playing on the school team.

Max and the kid have not seen each other in over a year. Chances are they'll never see each other again. Chances are also that the increasing demands of studenthood will usurp the kid's time for flinging a baseball with that good arm of his. It's probably just as well.

But somewhere out there, a skinny young man is walking around under a Chicago Cubs baseball cap. Although he may not look like much, he has faced the best hitters in both the Japanese and American major leagues. Max, no longer new to Japan, will not forget him. They went through a transition together, and had been pals.

The Toilet

THERE IS SOMETHING to be said for Japanese-style toilets. Just what that something is—or more particularly, just how to say it—may best be left to the experts in the bio/socio/anthropological/gymnastic fields of endeavor.

It is merely sufficient to report that the Japanese are more adept at handling basic exhaust functions at floor level than Westerners. In a way, that talent is more practical. It certainly is more natural.

Any elemental activity incorporating artifice as a matter of course, becomes after time, necessarily tied to the artifice. Old habits, as Plato once said, die hard. Without the artifice, which for Westerners in this case is a chair-height stool of porcelain, consternation develops. And consternation can be disconcerting.

Max Danger and a colleague from his office decided to build a ski house in the mountains. Serious Hirose, Section Chief, had inherited land in the Happo-one Mountain area of Nagano. With the statistically abnormal total of four children, Hirose had no money. Max, however, had a little money, plus a vague urge to develop economic equity in his host nation. He and Serious Hirose did a deal. Hirose ceded 20 percent of the land to Max who, in turn, funded the construction of the ski house. The house, surprisingly inexpensive to build, would be shared equally. Usage was determined by the "Saturday duty" office schedule.

178

Very few problems developed during the planning and construction phases of the project. Max and Hirose, of course, discussed the operation every few days. The entire Danger and Hirose families met twice to congratulate themselves on how well things were going. The beautiful Gloria and Mrs. Hirose communicated extensively in the seven words common to each other.

The trip to the Happo-one Mountains for the ground-breaking ceremony occurred during the first Danger winter in Japan. Everyone stayed at the Prince Hotel and fooled around on the ski slopes. Max never enjoyed himself more than he did that weekend.

Max's role in the venture was providing cash. Serious Hirose, meanwhile, knew that contractors and carpenters in the countryside were usually under-employed during the winter months, and he drove characteristically hard bargains with the various craftsmen involved in the project. Hirose obtained scheduling and material cost commitments which would make major Tokyo developers blush with shame. Max knew that the "*gaijin* partner" was a factor in the background of all Hirose's negotiations.

The house was finished on May 1. The Danger/Hirose Clans made the four-hour train trip to the mountains on May 2. The house was even better than the most optimistic expectations. Not fancy by any means, the structure was solid, had a serviceable kitchen, a fireplace of Max's design, and a lot of space in the loft for futons. It had floor-to-ceiling windows in the living room. It also had a large *ofuro* designed specially by a firm in Osaka. In a word, it was perfect.

Perfect except—and this, folks, is a large "except"—it had a Japanese toilet. Hmm. "Any elemental activity incorporating artifice, as a matter of course, becomes after time necessarily tied to the artifice." The beautiful Gloria,

179

and the Danger offspring, found the situation to be "difficult at best." There was always the Prince Hotel down the road, but that solution was not in all cases practical.

Something had to be done. Back in the office on Monday, Max and Serious Hirose discussed the issue. Hirose, to give him credit, was blessed with a degree of delicate sensitivity not always found in all gentlemen. "No problem," he said. "I arrange to fix at the fastest," he added.

And, by dammit, Hirose fixed it. A porcelain stool was ordered from Toto and sent to the mountains of Nagano. Workmen were implored, nay ordered, to install Western Machinery "at once." There was some talk of withholding final payment until the deed was done. Hirose received daily reports on the status of the plumbing "modifications."

On May 26, the Dangers again traveled to Happo-one—this time on their own. To walk into one's own house on a mountain slope anywhere, let alone in Japan, was a thrill. Max felt like a combination *daimyo,* eighteenth century British landlord, and an American entrepreneurial genius all rolled in one. It was beautiful.

Max's middle child, as was frequently the case, visited the toilet first. She was gone but a moment when her whoops and hollering began. She staggered from the room holding her sides. Hysterical laughter rendered her incapable of intelligent speech. All she could do was point back into the room. The family gathered.

A Western toilet was indeed in place. It was even color-coordinated with the light green tiles on the wall. The toilet seat was snugly fitted with a dark green terry-cloth covering, reflecting someone's concern about the long, cold winters in that part of the world. The hinge on the seat was well-machined—the seat flipped back and forth easily and soundlessly. Someone, the local plumber no doubt, had even placed freshly-cut flowers in a little vase on the tank.

The Dangers, nevertheless, dined that evening at the Prince Hotel. They incorporated artifice for any and all elemental activities.

The new Western toilet in the house—the toilet bowl specifically—had been recessed. The lip of the bowl, and the green-clad new seat, were at floor level!

A Real Adventure

MAX FROZE. On his left, across a small gully and up the gradually inclining hill, was a thicket of bushes. It had not been his imagination. Something in the bushes had moved.

The moon, still low in the sky even at midnight, cast shadows with light filtered by the branches of the surrounding trees. What little breeze there was could not have accounted for the rustling of the bushes.

Max's daughter, squeezing his hand even tighter, looked up.

"See, Daddy," she whispered, "there's something there."

"It's okay," said Max, knowing it probably wasn't.

As far as he could tell, Max and his daughter had been in shadows for the last five or six minutes. To make certain of their cover, he slowly backed himself and his daughter off the trail and closer to the trees on their right. They edged toward a large tree with a wide trunk—protecting one's rear is a basic commando tactic.

The thicket of bushes was still, but another movement behind the bushes and further up the hill caught Max's eye.

181

What appeared to be a branch seemed to be growing, as he watched, from a stand of a half-dozen small trees. It slowly dipped until it was horizontal to the ground. It was difficult to see, but the dark area at the base of the trees—which Max at first thought were more bushes—had gotten bigger.

Suddenly, and silently, the branch dropped out of sight. The reflected flash of moonlight as it dropped, however, left no doubt. It was the barrel of a rifle.

"Something's wrong here," Max whispered to his daughter. But she knew. It was her discovery of five or six minutes ago that had alerted them.

"Those bushes up there are moving across the ground," she had said.

"It's just the shadows caused by the moon," Max had replied.

They squatted on their haunches. Max realized his daughter was wearing her white Mickey Mouse sweatshirt—an item of apparel that had seldom been anywhere but on her since her birthday a month ago.

"Take off your sweatshirt, honey," Max whispered.

"But I'll be cold," she replied.

"The white is too easy to see."

Max took the sweatshirt and stuffed it under his own sweater. He unbuttoned his jacket and put it around his daughter's shoulders. Because they made the change with a minimum of sound and movement, the process took another two or three minutes.

Reconnoiter your immediate area, say the manuals. The trail they had just left bordered a pond which was about 25 meters across and roughly round, although a section of it seemed to narrow into what must have been a small stream running through the gully. If it was a stream, then the rustling bushes and the rifleman were on the other side of a natural barrier. Fine, except a bullet across the pond would

182

be obstructed by nothing but moonlight and fresh air.

Max looked back down the trail they had just traveled. "Holy Christ," he murmured, scaring his daughter even more. Two trees, not two meters from the edge of the trail, and not 15 meters from where they were squatting, became one. A man had just ducked for cover.

This can't be happening, Max thought to himself. But it sure as hell was. Would napalm come raining from the sky next? Nothing had prepared Max for being caught in the middle of something with his eight-year-old daughter.

"Do you see those big rocks over there?" Max asked his daughter softly. She nodded. The rocks were ahead of them, closer to the pond, but shrouded in shadows. They would provide cover from both the characters on the hill and whoever it was behind them.

"I'm going to throw a stone into the pond, and when it sploshes, we'll run to the rocks."

"Can you carry me, Daddy?"

"I'll carry you, honey."

Finding stones to do these kinds of things is easier in books than in real life. There were only pebbles in their immediate vicinity. Max and his daughter crept away from the safety of the big tree and back toward a mound of freshly upturned dirt. They were careful to avoid the patches of dappled moonlight splattered here and there on the ground. Max found a stone.

Turning to throw, Max stopped. Someone, in the darkness across the gully, was running. The crunch of footsteps, not a loud sound ordinarily, filled the air. Then a cracking, snapping crash. Someone, it sounded, had jumped *into* a thicket of bushes.

"Baka," rang across the pond.

And then silence.

Max and his daughter waited.

183

"Are they *really* after us, Daddy?" she whispered.

A good point, thought Max. Whatever was happening didn't seem to bring anyone closer to them. Max looked back down the trail—at the tree behind which someone had hidden earlier—but no one, as far as he could tell, was there.

Max threw the stone. He picked up his daughter and was already running as the stone splashed in the pond. Someone whistled—a brief, shrill blast. Max jumped behind the rocks.

The scream—"AEIIIYAAA"—scared the bejesus out of Max. His daughter yelled and, judging by the condition of his throat afterwards, so did Max.

His first thought was that they had landed on an alligator. It was brown, and was wriggling on its belly. Max flipped it over.

There, staring up at Max and his daughter, was one terrified Japanese man. He was wearing, get ready for this, a Third Reich German military combat uniform.

Within seconds, the area by the pond in Arisugawa Park—yes, *that* park—was illuminated by at least a dozen men with flashlights. They were all wearing military uniforms. Most of the uniforms were Japanese, but there was the German one, and some that looked definitely American.

Apologies flew. Embarrassment was rampant. The "combatants," all middle-aged Japanese salaryman-types, were playing a war game! It was, for them, a more or less regular club event. (Their guns, as demonstrated to the delight of Max's daughter, shot "bullets" of soft chalk that left red stains on the uniforms of their victims. The guns were spring-loaded.)

Well, it's difficult to be too critical, as guests, of the practices of those in a host nation. War games, after all, were very popular a few years ago on U.S. university campuses.

184

Max accepted the apologies, reluctantly at first, and then with an attempt at good humor. (A crate of melons was later sent to his apartment with additional apologies.)

His daughter chattered merrily all the way home. It had been for her great fun. Max didn't feel quite as good.

"Were you scared, Daddy?" asked an obviously relieved little girl as they entered Homat Cornucopia.

"Yes, honey," replied Max after a while, "I was."

The Secretary

"BEHIND EVERY successful man is a something or other woman."

Max Danger firmly believes in the spirit of the quotation even though he's not certain of its exact wording. The general concept, that women really Run The Show, is, however, valid.

Many otherwise impressive figures—captains of industry, pillars of the community, leaders of state—could not find their shoes in the morning, or remember to eat leafy green vegetables, without the firm guidance of the feminine hand. Left to their own devices, men would still be wearing beaver skins, painting themselves blue, and puzzling over puberty initiation rites around the campfire.

The Japan Experience, for expats in business, brings this point home. Another woman, however, enters the picture. None of us could really function, whether we like it or not, without The Secretary.

Of course, The Secretary back home was important. How

else would expense accounts get processed and alibis be confirmed? And who, but The Secretary, could refrain from putting a bullet in the boss's skull after hearing, "Hell, Sam, my secretary must have screwed-up—I put the check in the mail to you last week," once too often?

But back home, The Secretary merely keeps the boss out of jail. In Japan, The Secretary keeps the expat, and for a while his family, alive!

Most international school applications and enrollments are handled by The Secretary. She obtains all club memberships. The Secretary negotiates with landlords, building superintendents, the misfits in the company General Affairs Department, the Drivers' License Bureau, the Ward Office, and the oriental carpet salesmen. All of that, plus the normal business routine. ("*Sumimasen,* Watanabe-san, my secretary must have screwed-up—I put the check in the mail to you last week.")

The above is meant to emphasize Max's awareness of, and appreciation for, the vital role played by an expat's Secretary. If it weren't for Max's own Secretary, for example, these little stories would never see the light of day. Although it's probably thrilling for her to come to the office early in the morning to type these—or even more exciting to bang them out during her lunch hour—there is still a "beyond the call of duty" aspect about it. (And, incidentally, aren't these pieces extremely well-typed and punctuated?)

Now, the point is that language difficulties and cultural differences *do* create amusing "situational events." Max collects these stories and offers them, with modest suggestions as to how to avoid terminal apoplexy, to the expat business community.

BE CAREFUL OF COLLOQUIALISMS I: "Your wife is dead," stated the note handed to an expat accountant as he

186

emerged from a two-hour meeting. "Please call up to your friend," it continued. One can imagine the panic engulfing the expat. Except his wife answered the phone when he called home. What on earth? Later in the morning, a pal phoned the accountant. "Did you get my message?" he asked. "I told The Secretary to get you out of the meeting before lunch. I told her it was a matter of 'Life and Death'."

BE CAREFUL OF COLLOQUIALISMS II: "It's too bad about your pets," a customer said, as Max arrived late for a meeting. The meeting did not go well. The customer was not his cheerful, purchasing self. At the conclusion of the meeting, the customer told Max to hurry back to his animals. It took some time to puzzle out what had happened. The customer had been given a note saying that Max would be late because his dog and cat were wet. Max, of course, had phoned ahead saying he'd be late because of traffic conditions. "It's raining cats and dogs," he had told The Secretary.

BE CAREFUL OF COLLOQUIALISMS III: "Please call to Mr. Sarbastin," said The Secretary's note. "The grapes told him you have to go." "Sarbastin" turned out to be "Silverstein." Fair enough. The "grapes" remained a mystery. It wasn't until much later—when Silverstein used the expression again—that comprehension dawned. A transfer back to the States was being considered, and Silverstein had heard about it "on the grapevine."

BE PARTICULARLY EXPLICIT WITH INSTRUCTIONS: The new expat's predecessor was a man of effete and civilized tastes. He drank coffee from a tidy little *demitasse*. (And, no doubt, stirred the coffee with tidy little fingers.) The new expat was heavier on quantity than quality. Larger cups, however, were not immediately available. "Bring me two cups," demanded our hero. "Cream and sugar," he added. The Secretary brought the two cups—one with coffee and cream, one with coffee and sugar.

BE PARTICULARLY EXPLICIT WITH INSTRUCTIONS II: "Photocopy the paper-clipped pages," instructed the new man. He had been up most of the night before, reading through corporate manuals. Several hundred pages of particularly key instructions were to be condensed for the benefit of local staff. The paper-clips were to separate the wheat from the chaff, so to speak. The Secretary handled the job. She could not be faulted. The sequence of words, unfortunately, did not register. She handed the new expat, after twenty minutes or so, a page of photo-copied paper-clips—carefully removed from the manuals and reproduced.

DON'T EVEN ATTEMPT JAPANESE UNTIL YOU'RE CERTAIN: "I'm horny," announced the new expat to The Secretary at the conclusion of his first day in the office. "And I need your help," he continued. It took almost a week, and two union meetings, to sort out the conflicting interpretations of the affair. The Secretary had asked the new expat to sign the pink copy of a multi-copy marine insurance declaration form. The expat, color-blind from birth, revealed his affliction *(shikimo desu)*. As fate would have it, the expat's pronounciation was a little shaky—particularly toward the the end of the word. *Shikima desu* means "passionately aroused." They're still talking about that around the office.

SPELL YOUR NAME: The Sarbastin/Silverstein situation is mentioned above. Consider poor Lloyd Falley. No one returned his phone calls for the 3.8 years he lived in Japan.

Barry Phair is considering a lawsuit. And if your name is Rudy Fachtmann—change it.

RETAIN A SENSE OF HUMOR REGARDING MESSAGES (AFTER ALL, LIFE WILL PROBABLY GO ON):
"Please to call Mr. Kuwarku (Krack ???!!??) His number 424–?361(424–361?)."

Or, "Down is the garage. Your car."

Or, "We don't the meeting. You go home."

Or, "If not, call him to say before 4:00."

Or, "Number is 216–6611, Mr.? cannot wait."

Or, "We did not tell to him because of your away. However seems mad. Call back please. Maybe long distance."

Or, "Hoshina-san said its not to pay but you don't know him. Weather information."

Or, "From the Embassy. Its okay, (Or call back)."

Or, "Johnson. Because of taxes (Texas?)"

APPRECIATE THE EFFORT: The new expat inherited The Secretary, who herself had just been elevated to the position, replacing a lady retiring after thirty years with the company. For the purposes of general office organization, the new expat asked The Secretary to file his predecessor's collection of business cards alphabetically by company. There were several thousand of them. The project, to be worked on during odd moments in the day, could take months. The new expat jet-lagged into the office early the next morning. The Secretary was asleep on the floor under his conference table. She had spent the night—and completed the project.

Depending on Circumstances, Nakedness Can Be Embarrassing

MOST PEOPLE are naked at some time or other during each 24-hour period. It is, after all, the natural state.

Unless one is addicted to "limited zone" sponge-bathing, or extended camping trips amongst the creatures of the forest, getting naked is an ordinarily regular event in our daily lives. As it should be.

Seeing oneself naked in the mirror, as the shower steam clears, is not particularly embarrassing. It may be distressing—the diet mightn't be catching on as planned—but it's not embarrassing.

In fact, honesty dictates occasional, but serious, appraisals of our naked selves. Random bulges, unexplained hollows, skin eruptions, and the cruel effects of gravity may require some attention.

Who of us would wish to learn from a perfect stranger that his or her backside sports a rash which in configuration resembles the profile of Wilkie Collins, famous 19th century author and scholar?

And who, save the most commited masochist, wishes to hear that sumo's Mr. Konishiki—he of the awesome girth—possesses breast development more spectacular than that currently under consideration? If you're a woman, that is.

But never mind. Appearing naked in front of others can be perfectly normal and not at all embarrassing. One assumes most husbands and wives have mastered their reactions in this regard. Athletes showering together treat the situation with a casualness that is positively healthy. (Max, having once run in a track meet in East Germany, showered happily with fellow competitors, only to learn later that one-fifth of his shower-mates were subsequent participants in international women's track and field events. Try as he might, Max could not remember any specifics which should have alerted him.)

In Japan, it appears that nakedness has traditionally been more "accepted" as a condition of life than it has in the West. The Japanese have not had the advantage of knowing culturally about Adam and Eve's intense shame over their own nakedness after The Fall. It's a pity. In fact, it wasn't until the historically recent influx of outsiders that the Japanese saw the Error Of Their Ways and discouraged public mixed bathing and other wicked things.

It should be said parenthetically that Max, as a Western-er, *does* have difficulty imagining an innocent society of folks romping together in rice paddies by day, and splashing together in communal baths by night. The statures of the young ladies in his Accounting Department cloud his mind in this respect and refute the anthropological argument offered by some *gaijin* that the physical differences between the sexes in Japan are of the merest variations in the theme of humanity—a blip here, a blap without a blip there.

What is of concern is that Max Danger, for a period of about 30 seconds, appeared stark raving, day-of-birth na-tural, innocent-in-the-garden naked before a thousand or so people in the Ginza. At 3:00 in the afternoon, on a Saturday. And he believes by *his* standards, he was em-barrassed.

Max likes sumo. Many foreigners do. The sport is con-ceptually simple in performance, but subtly complex in execution. It's fun to watch; it's easy to analyze.

191

One of Max's friends had been dangerously close to going "over the edge" as a sumo fan for several years. He visited stables, he went to matches, he collected sumo prints, his office was filled with sumo knick-knacks, he taped daytime matches for night-time viewing, and he even got himself invited to Grand Champion Chiyonofuji's wedding. He was, in a word, hooked.

He also got transferred—back to the States. "Wouldn't it be fun," thought Max to himself, "to show up at his *sayonara* party wearing a *mawashi?*"

> "Stomp, stomp on the floor
> As he's opening the door."

"I'll do it," Max confirmed to himself. "And I'll give him the *mawashi* as a *sayonara* present after the party."

Easier said than done, however. A *mawashi* is a long strip of cloth—usually made of silk—which comprises the sole costume worn by sumo wrestlers during their matches. Intricate wrapping and folding techniques are employed to guarantee a modicum of modesty whilst simultaneously providing offensive/defensive grip opportunities for maneuvers.

Are there stores for these things? Unlike tennis shorts and golf shoes, *mawashi* do not appear on display in your average *spotsu shoppu*.

Max assigned the task of finding a *mawashi* to Watanabe-san of his General Affairs Department. Watanabe-san, whose time would otherwise be spent picking his teeth, perusing his personal porno collection, or renewing the annual insurance policy on Max's company car, accepted the assignment with alacrity. "It's going up to my alley," he declared.

Watanabe-san came through. A friend of a relative's friend's friend, who was a bartender in "downtown" Tokyo, obtained a *mawashi*. It wouldn't be silk, Watanabe-san reported, but it would be "more or less cotton."

Picking up the *mawashi,* and being instructed on how to wear it, involved a process typically Japanese—and typically complex. The "product" passed through many hands. Max wondered, but never asked, how much of the purchase price actually applied to the *mawashi* and how much applied to the delivery system.

Nevertheless, the deal was agreed upon and arranged. Max went to the office on Saturday and picked Watanabe-san up at noon. They had a bite to drink for lunch—in fact several bites—and toddled off arm in arm to a department store in the Ginza. A friend of the neighbor of the bartender, who had obtained the *mawashi,* worked at the department store in the Young Men's and Fine Handsome Dept. He knew how to wrap and secure a *mawashi*.

Since the "fitting" had nothing to do with the Young Men's and Fine Handsome Dept., an alternate venue had been arranged. Space, for tightly wrapping a five meter-long piece of cloth around the body, was also a consideration. Max, Watanabe-san, and the clerk furtively slipped off and returned to the main floor of the department store.

They entered a room in the front part of the building. Except for stray body parts of mannikins scattered amongst scraps of cloth on the floor, the room was empty. Plain brown paper was taped across the length and breadth of one wall.

Ordinarily a model of modesty and decorum, Max was nevertheless persuaded to strip. *Mawashi*-fitting starts from scratch, so to speak. (If the truth were known, Max *did* have some misgivings about whether or not random bits of his anatomy would be decently encompassed by the between-the-legs looping of the costume. After all, sumo wrestlers are, or might be, built differently.)

It was probably a combination of nervous embarrassment on everyone's part, plus the cumulative effect of the luncheon cocktails, that caused the participants in the drama to find the proceedings to be somewhat more than mildly amusing. Watanabe-san, face aglow, was particularly sensitive to the humor in the situation. Of course, Max didn't help any by pirouetting with exaggerated grace as the wrapping of the garment around the body progressed. Dealing for the first time with a foreigner up close, as the clerk certainly was, may have contributed to the instability of the moment. False starts frequently brought the process back to square one.

Max now remembers it all clearly. He remembers slapping his face and pounding his chest as if preparing for a bout. He remembers Watanabe-san finding this to be particularly hilarious. Max also remembers the clerk struggling with the end-tuck—the crucial anchoring of the *mawashi* within the wrapped folds. He remembers the clerk not getting it right.

Max remembers wiping under his arms with an imaginary cloth and then wiping his face. He remembers these gestures dissolving Watanabe-san in hysterics. He remembers watching Watanabe-san reel backwards, almost in slow motion, against the wall that ran the length of the room. Max remembers watching the brown paper, tape and all, being ripped from the wall as Watanabe-san slid to the floor.

Max remembers the clerk leaping away from him as if zapped by megavolts of electricity. He remembers watching the *mawashi* slowly unwind and assemble itself in loose coils around his ankles. Max remembers how silent it suddenly became in the room.

Max also remembers wondering fleetingly if the tendency to freeze in moments of panic is the same mechanism in humans as it appears to be in the wild animals who stand transfixed by the headlights of approaching automobiles.

Max, most of all, remembers the knocking on the wall. He remembers how it took a while for his brain to register the fact that he was *watching* the person who was knocking on the wall. And that person was *outside* the wall!

Well, there may not have been "thousands" of people strolling on the sidewalk past the Ginza department store display window—probably only "hundreds." And Max may not have been standing entranced for thirty seconds—probably closer to twenty.

But once the ability to act was restored, the window shoppers and earnest citizenry on the streets of Ginza never saw a pair of trousers donned more rapidly. The trousers were inside out, and there was an unprintable problem with the zipper, but we're talking world-record rapid.

And you know, Max *was* embarrassed by the whole thing.

Author's Note: Whilst "poetic licence" permits the adjustment of facts to enhance drama, the author nevertheless feels compelled to report that Max was not exactly naked in the window. He was wearing over-the-calf blue business socks.

Snowbound, Part I

MAX WAS NOT even certain when the car went off the road.

In a way, he was relieved as it crunched to a halt against the snowbank. His vision through the windshield for the last forty minutes had been reduced to a tunnel the width of the car and extending only a few feet beyond the hood.

Snow swirled so wildly that it was impossible to tell how much was actually falling and how much was being blown up from the ground. It was a serious storm.

Max had been following increasingly vague tracks on what he supposed to be a road—his only clue in this regard had been the flickering red tail lights of some fool in a car up ahead. Those lights gradually disappeared, as did the lights of the car behind him.

Now, submerged in snow the height of his fenders, Max sat back in his seat. He had the distinct feeling his car would not move again until the spring thaw.

"Are we stuck?" asked the beautiful Gloria, whose ability to cite the obvious was matched only by a talent for it putting it in question form.

"We should have waited until morning," suggested the oldest Danger offspring, whose plans for video-gaming had been disrupted by the evening departure.

"We should have left this afternoon," countered the middle Danger child, whose friends were returning from vacation early the next morning.

"I have to go big toilet," announced the youngest, whose activity in that regard had ceased four days ago.

The Dangers had been on a skiing holiday in Nagano. They were now somewhere in the mountains and, to all appearances, quite alone.

"I'll look around," announced Max, pushing his way out of the car. He slipped getting out, nearly fell under the vehicle, plowed through knee-high drifts, and stumbled back to the road. He looked around.

Nothing. Clearly traffic had stopped for the duration of the blizzard. Snow was falling even faster than Max had realized. The tracks his car had made were beginning to fill. They would be gone in a matter of minutes.

Up ahead and to the right, Max glimpsed a light during brief interludes in the snowy maelstrom. Something was there—a port in a storm, so to speak.

"There may be a place we can go," Max stated, as he returned to the warmth of car and family. "It's up ahead, and can't be more than a mile or so away."

The family, meanwhile, was debating the wisdom of Max's decision to leave the ski lodge for Tokyo in the middle of the night. It was a few moments before he gained their attention.

"But we'll have to walk there," he reported, once order was restored. The statement set off another round of debate.

Finally the family Danger was persuaded that nothing was to be gained by remaining where they were, save a slow death by freezing, asphyxiation, or both. Snow could conceivably bury the car in an hour or so.

Everyone was urged to select his or her warmest items of apparel from the car's trunk. Max attempted to inject a sense of fun into the proceedings.

"Let's pretend we're explorers discovering new and uncharted territories," he suggested.

"What do you mean 'pretend'," Gloria responded. Her mood, for some reason, was as dark as the night.

The first ten or fifteen minutes of the hike toward the light in the woods was actually exhilarating. One of nature's most glorious displays must be the phenomenon of heavy snow in a mountainside forest. Evergreens, branches heavy with the burden of new-fallen fluff, droop in poetic elegance. Harsh sounds are muffled. Each step is an adventure into an unknown and virginal world—a world where man has not before traveled. The experience is most certainly primordial.

It also makes your feet cold. And your nose run. Branches, slung low, shower snow down one's neck. Buried and therefore invisible traps of webbed undergrowth can send adventurers sprawling. The realities of terrain variations, particularly in the dark, are cunningly disguised by the misleadingly benign blanket of nature's whitewash. And, in a mountainside forest, it can be all uphill.

"The light's not getting any closer," reported Max's daughter after thirty minutes.

"Yes, it is," wheezed Max. "It can't, logically, be running away from us."

"But it sure as hell is more than a mile from here," confirmed Gloria, using language heretofore unheard from her lips. The family grunted assent, and plowed onward and upward.

One hour and thirteen minutes later, the Dangers stumbled into a broad open area, which indicated signs of human cultivation. At the end of an expanse about the size of an American football field, a farmhouse loomed. With snow piled high on the roof, it looked like a Fred Harris painting—cozy, but closed to outsiders. A spotlight glared across the open field.

The march across the field to the house was as exhausting as any part of the trip. Unhindered by trees, snow had fallen and accumulated with a vengeance. It was uniformly thigh-deep for Max, and it meant that he and Gloria had to carry the two younger children. Progress was measured in paces—a dozen steps, and then a rest for a minute or two.

Everything below Max's knees registered pain, Gloria's feet had gone numb a half-hour ago, and their youngest was experiencing severe discomfort over the "big toilet" issue. What had started as a semi-lark, was becoming a very basic struggle for survival. They were within twenty yards of the farmhouse when the light went out.

"Hurry up, Dad," said Max's oldest. "They're going to bed." Indeed, it must have been after 1:30 A.M.

Max, with his daughter in his arms, reached the house first. The structure was wooden with a real thatched roof. Odd sizes and colors of boards seemed to be randomly slapped on to the walls, as if a hasty patchwork job had been completed minutes before. Nevertheless, light from the inside of the house shone in several places through cracks in the exterior of the building.

Max stared at the white rectangular plaque announcing the owner's name. It would be nice to be able to read the kanji. But then again, it would be even nicer to be able to say "Save my family" in the owner's language. Gloria and the rest of the Dangers plowed up behind.

"Hurry, Daddy," said the youngest.

"Hang on, kid," Max advised. "You can go to the toilet in a minute."

He pounded on the door. A dog, or perhaps two dogs, erupted inside. Between barks, Max could hear shuffling steps approaching the door. A gust of wind swirled snow around the Dangers, as if nature was making its last attack.

A young lady opened the door. Over her shoulder, Max could see into the interior of the house. About a half-dozen people were sitting around a low table watching television. He had the impression that an open fire was glowing in a grate set against the far wall. The observations took but a second—yet Max was immediately convinced that paradise meant a warm, dry farmhouse occupied by startled peasants in the wilds of Nagano.

The young lady was wearing jeans and a turtle-neck sweater. Her hair was swept back and tied in a ponytail. She was wearing just the slightest hint of pink lipstick. A silver chain, with a dangling medallion, girded her waist. Her fingernails were bright red.

"Danger-san," said the young lady, "what are *you* doing *here?*"

199

Snowbound, Part II

AH YES, FOLKS, it is indeed a small world. ("Of all the gin mills, in all the cities, of all the world—," Bogie said to Ingrid as she showed up at Rick's American Café in downtown Casablanca.)

Small world encounters, nevertheless, are usually fun. They bring people together who might otherwise never meet again—high school teachers now in the diplomatic corps, old sweethearts married to tycoons (or to bums), the neighborhood buffoon teaching philosophy at Sophia, or second cousins disguised as British currency traders.

Small world encounters usually occur, however, in situations which are not all that remarkable. Standing around in an international hotel lobby for any length of time significantly increases the chances of running into an old acquaintance. (Americans formerly claimed that everyone you've ever known passes through Grand Central Station.) Max once met an old track coach negotiating balance of trade payments with several young ladies in a Tijuana, Mexico night spot.

These encounters occur because the people involved are out and around, and moving in public areas frequented by millions. The encounters happen—but the joy of recognition usually tempers any discomfort attendant to the occasion.

Bursting in on simple, isolated country folk in the middle

of the night can be socially awkward, however. Bursting in on simple, isolated country folk in the middle of the night without the ability to speak their language can be even more difficult. Bursting in on simple, isolated country folk in the middle of the night without the ability to speak their language and then seeing a familiar face, can be mind-blowing.

Max knocked on the farmhouse door.

"Danger-san," said the young lady answering the door in rural Nagano-ken, "what are *you* doing *here?*"

Max's mouth opened, but no words came out.

"And who those people with you?" continued the young lady at the farmhouse door. "By the way," she added, "I still save your necktie."

Well, ladies and gentlemen, we often go through life overlooking, or not registering, the obvious. Yet it is all very simple. Roppongi bar hostesses *must* come from families living somewhere.

"Ah, Kristie," Max managed to say after swallowing twice.

"My name here is Kazuko," interrupted Kristie.

"Ah, Kazuko," continued Max, "my family, that is, my *wife* and *three children* are out here slowly freezing to death."

"Why?"

"Because, Kristie, our car—"

"Kazuko."

"Because, Kazuko, our car went off the road and is now stuck in the snow," Max explained.

"Can we come in?" asked the youngest Danger, bringing the issue to a head. "I have to go big toilet."

With that, the five Dangers began a two-day New Year's holiday with Kristie/Kazuko Hirano, her parents, two grandparents, a sister, the sister's husband, their two children, an unmarried brother, an "uncle" (or friend), and two elderly ladies from a neighboring farm.

201

Those were the humans. Sharing the modest facilities were two cows (housed and being fattened in a shed attached and partially open to the "family room"), two dogs, two cats, five chickens roaming amongst the cows' legs, and a hyperactive frog named "Beat."

The house, all on one floor, consisted of three bedrooms, a kitchen, a storage room (in which the elderly neighbor ladies seemed to have set up camp), and the "family room." No, the toilet is not mistakenly omitted from the description of the house. It was outside—attached to the house, but outside. (The youngest Danger endured his private agony until noon of the following day.)

After introductions, and a great deal of conversation in Japanese, the Dangers were welcomed with arms as open as space allowed. They were implored to sit immediately at the *kotatsu*—a low table with a heater in the recessed area beneath it. Gloria and the kids were given hot tea. Max was served a glass of home-made saké which had the subtlety of a steam locomotive and the "character" of molten lava. It was bloody marvelous.

Kristie/Kazuko handled all translations. Max was, to her family, a "business associate" from Tokyo; to Gloria, Max was her "most favorite customer ever" in a Roppongi Club. ("The American Club?" asked the youngest Danger.)

Conversation mercifully waned after about an hour. Sleeping arrangements were agreed upon. Quite simply, the Dangers joined Kristie/Kazuko, her brother, and the "uncle" (friend) on the "family room" floor. Keeping them company were one of the dogs, the cows and their pals, the chickens. Max decided against making a witty remark to Gloria about it being the first time he'd ever slept with a bar hostess.

It took a day-and-a-half for the snow plows to clear the road. It took several hours to dig the Danger automobile out of the mountain of snow left by the plows. The Dangers and Hiranos, therefore, spent a great amount of time very much together.

SOME OBSERVATIONS:
Country folk are indeed hospitable and accommodating. The elderly neighbor ladies had been staying with the Hiranos for two months. Something was wrong with their roof, and plans were being made to fix it in the spring. The "uncle" (friend) had been living with the Hiranos since 1971.

Country folk, mountain farmers that is, do absolutely nothing all winter. The house had three television sets—two of them hooked up to video games. The wake/sleep cycle is totally controlled by the hours of T.V. broadcasting.

The details of life in the big city, as they apply to an attractive daughter, are generally unknown. Or at least, not re-marked upon. For about seven years, the Hiranos thought Kristie/Kazuko was a student in Tokyo. This, despite the fact that during one of Mrs. Hirano's infrequent trips to see Kristie/Kazuko, she discovered more beaded gowns in her daughter's closet than one could possibly rationalize as being standard student garb. They now think Kristie/Kazuko is a successful nurse. Which is why she can afford to live in Akasaka.

Living close to the earth, with a lot of people (and animals) around, tends to focus humor on the basics. Some of the more amusing moments occurring during the Danger visit had to do with sounds emanating from the toilet—outdoors, but attached to the house. One of the elderly neighbor ladies was particularly adept at causing mirth within the group watching television in the "family room." Her visits to the toilet,

203

which were remarkably often, would usually create rafter-rattling sonic booms impossible to ignore. She would always take the obviously good-natured jibes—which Kristie/Kazuko never translated—in the proper spirit.

Country folk, particularly those never having seen foreigners up close, invariably wonder where the hair is. One of the earliest *gaijiin* to visit Japan must have been exceptionally hairy. His hirsute characteristics apparently entered folk-lore in a big way. The Hiranos were astonished to discover that the Dangers were less hairy than they.

A great deal of political power is attributed to the Imperial Family. Despite countless hours in front of the T.V., solutions to national problems were perceived to be in the hands of the Emperor, not the "smooth one" (Prime Minister Nakasone). Of great concern were the marriage plans of Prince Hiro. Kristie/Kazuko's grandmother had saved over one hundred magazine articles on the subject.

One liter of home-made saké can fuel a 747 to Hawaii and back. Max considered pouring some on his frozen automobile engine. He went to bed the second evening in Nagano convinced he'd awake in the morning blind.

Little finger games and tricks with matches, performed by bar hostesses in the daytime for the amusement of children, are not as hilarious as they appear in club surroundings late at night. Max felt obliged to censor a number of Kristie/Kazuko's stunts.

Cows eat, and process through their systems, great quantities of food each day. "There they go again," Max's youngest would announce regularly, once his own big toilet issue had been resolved. Never having lived on a farm, Max's youngest made the announcement several dozen times a day. He held the cows in awe.

When you stop and think about it, two days is a long time for bar hostesses and wives to spend together chatting. If it hadn't been for the home-made saké, Max may never have slept.

One can get used to teeth of gold. Max even began wondering what his own bicuspids would look like trimmed in yellow.

Country folk—with whom several days are spent lolling on the floor, eating omochi, chewing dried fish, listening to the antics of elderly neighbor ladies, and unavoidably rubbing against—can be suprisingly sentimental. The entire group, save a slightly infirm grandfather, made the trek down to the Danger automobile to see the family off. Word that the Dangers made it safely back to Tokyo was to be relayed through Kristie/Kazuko, who was staying in Nagano one more day. The youngest Danger promised to send a new video game to one of the nephews. The red-cheeked grandmother wiped tears from her eyes as the car slid on its way.

"What was that about Kristie/Kazuko saving your necktie?" asked Gloria, as the waving and "bye-byes" ceased.
    "I must have taken it off at the club," replied Max, steering the car carefully.
    "Why?"
    "It's a cramped, stuffy little place on the second floor of

205

an old building in Roppongi. I really wouldn't go there," Max continued, "except it's a safe and reasonably inexpensive place to bring clients."

"Maybe Kristie/Kazuko won't have to work there much longer," Gloria said after a few moments.

"Oh?"

"I'm arranging for her to give Japanese lessons to the ladies in my American Club exercise class."

Max swerved the car suddenly, narrowly avoiding a patch of ice on the road.